A SHERLOCK HOLMES NOTEBOOK
A Cornucopia of Sherlockania
BY GARY LOVISI

STARK
HOUSE

Stark House Press • Eureka California

A SHERLOCK HOLMES NOTEBOOK

Published by Stark House Press
1315 H Street
Eureka, CA 95501, USA
griffinskye3@sbcglobal.net
www.starkhousepress.com

ISBN: 978-1-951473-91-4

Book design by Mark Shepard, shepgraphics.com

First Stark House Press Edition: May 2022

A SHERLOCK HOLMES NOTEBOOK

Gary Lovisi has been collecting Sherlock Holmes arcana for decades, and has written on every aspect of the Great Detective and the literary world of Sir Arthur Conan Doyle. He has collected 22 of those articles in this profusely illustrated edition that celebrates the joys and discovery of collecting.

It's all here: from the scarce paperbacks to the classic hardcovers; the films, the comics, and the magazines... Holmes on stage and screen... the rare Mexican Sherlock Holmes series... the Penzler Sherlock Holmes Library... even Professor Challenger and the Lost World make an appearance! Lovisi writes about the pastiches, the fan writings, the scholarly musings... even the Sherlock Holmes cards!

If you are fan of Holmes, a book collector, a lover of Victorian London, or simply curious about this fascinating world of homage and detection, this is the book for you. Gary Lovisi offers a cornucopia of Sherlockania in this Sherlock Holmes Notebook!

The New Adventures of
SHERLOCK HOLMES

Original Stories by Eminent Mystery Writers

Edited by Martin Harry Greenberg and
Carol-Lynn Rössel Waugh

CENTENNIAL EDITION AUTHORIZED
BY THE CONAN DOYLE ESTATE

CONTENTS

Introduction:
A Cornucopia of Sherlockania

This book contains two of my passions; my love of everything Sherlock Holmes, and the joys and discovery of collecting; especially book collecting — hardcovers and paperbacks. However, that is not all.

Sherlock Holmes is a timeless character and one avidly collected today in a host of venues — films, art, comic books, cards, magazines, but especially books. So you will find a variety of those items throughout this book.

Holmes, Watson, Victorian London, and other aspects of 'The Canon' are also items that fans and scholars have written numerous articles, essays and even entire books about — just for the fun of it — just for the love of Holmes! Some of those articles I have included here and I hope you will find their topics intriguing.

I've been bitten by the Holmes bug for quite a few decades now, fascinated by Doyle's original stories, amused by the pastiches, enjoying the fannish and scholarly non-fiction musings. And I, as have many others, have written various articles (as well as pastiche stories and novels), that express my own joy and interest in the Great Detective and the books about him and other Doyle creations. In this new book from Stark House Press you will find articles that run the gamut of Holmes collectables in book form. Scarce paperback editions, and classic hardcovers, as well as many of the pastiches and some series are in this book. Obviously, you will find some old friends and items that many Sherlockians are familiar with, but also some items that you may not be familiar with at all. One aspect of being a Holmes collector is the sheer joy of discovery, and I hope this book whets the appetite and offers new and interesting items for the fan and collector who may wish to delve further into all things related to Sherlock Holmes and Sir Arthur Conan Doyle.

These articles were fun for me to research and to write, and I hope they are fun for you to read. And if you experience that joy of discovery in reading about these items then I have done my job. I hope you enjoy this notebook presenting a cornucopia of Sherlockania.

Gary Lovisi
Brooklyn, New York
January 6, 2022

Sherlock Holmes:
The Early Hardcover Pastiche Firsts!

I: The Early Pastiches

Sherlock Holmes… The very name conjures up the magic of mystery and detection, hansom cabs, foggy London streets, Victorian crime… and Watson! And Professor Moriarity! All weaved together by master writer Sir Arthur Conan Doyle.

Such was the incredible popularity of Doyle's detective that the public created an almost insatiable demand, a demand Doyle could not fill – even during his lifetime. A demand, that in time, the author no longer wanted to fill.

Doyle grew tired of chronicling the stories of his popular detective hero, who he felt was taking him away from more serious works. Even as Sherlock Holmes practically became a 'person' in his own right – or was so perceived by much of the reading public – Doyle saw only one solution and finally killed off Holmes at the Richenbach Falls. However, the clamor of public outcry was too great, and publisher renumeration so vast, Doyle had to bring Holmes back to life. Doyle eventually relented and continued to chronicle Holmes' adventures in more books and further issues of the *Strand Magazine.*

With Doyle's death in 1930, Sherlock and 'the Canon' or what dedicated Sherlockians also call 'the sacred writings'— being only those original stories written by Doyle — have been added to, and continued in parody, pastiche, and story form by a dedicated group of diverse hands. Of the many books that contain novels, short story collections, or anthologies *not* written by Doyle, there have been many fine

and fascinating additions over the years. Sherlockia, always
an interesting area for collectors and dealers, is even more
interesting with regard to the wide array of hardcover
pastiche Firsts having been written over the decades from
the 1960s to the 1990s. These books have really taken off and
recently some very talented writers have carved out their
own personal niche in Sherlockia with their own characters
based in some way on the Canon.

Even during Doyle's lifetime various Holmes imitators
appeared and flourished, such was the unparalleled
popularity of the Great Detective. These early imitators of
Holmes appeared in parodies and pastiches under a plethora
of Holmes-sounding names to avoid copyright infringement.
One such was Herlock Sholmes created by Peter Todd and
published early this century in various magazine short
stories. These stories were eventually collected decades later
as *The Adventures of Herlock Sholmes* (Mysterious Press,
1976) in a special 1250 copy edition, wherein 250 were
signed and numbered by famed science fiction author Philip
Jose Farmer, who wrote the introduction. This is just one
example of what I call the 'pseudo-Sherlock pastiches.' It
was Sherlock, usually in everything but name, but still not
exactly Holmes. Another example are the fine books by
Robert L. Fish chronicling the adventures of his Holmes
parody, Skerlock Holes. Great fun but still more parody than
actual pastiche, and as such, outside the scope of this article.

One of the earliest pastiches that skirted the Holmes
mythos, without actually entering it fully, was Anthony
Boucher's classic crime novel *The Case of The Baker Street
Irregulars* (Simon & Schuster, 1940). This was a fine murder
mystery with a Sherlockian flavor that is one of the classic
books that kept the memory of the Great Detective alive
until actual pastiches with him in them by name could legally
be written. In this one a Hollywood studio is filming a Doyle
classic when there is murder and other odd happenings to be
investigated in the best Sherlockian manner.

What happens when Sherlock Holmes meets Houdini in
The
ADVENTURE OF
THE ECTOPLASMIC
MAN
A SHERLOCK HOLMES MYSTERY
DANIEL
STASHOWER

The Adventure
of the Stalwart
Companions
Edited and annotated by
H. Paul Jeffers

Heretofore unpublished letters and papers
concerning a singular collaboration between
Theodore Roosevelt and Sherlock Holmes

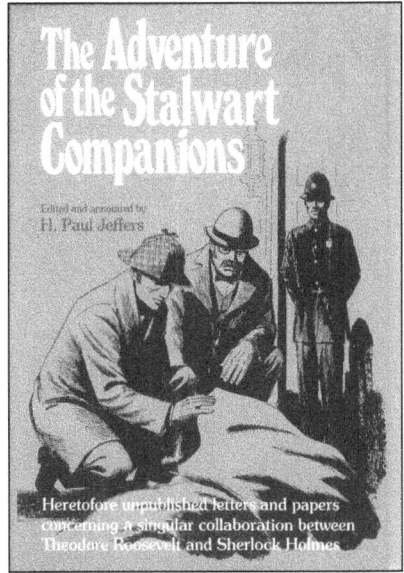

However, it didn't take very long for that first book of *new* pastiches to appear. One of the earliest Sherlock Holmes pastiche anthologies appeared in 1944. The book that broke this new ground and caused some consternation was, *The Misadventures of Sherlock Holmes*, edited by Ellery Queen (Little Brown & Co., March, 1944), featuring a stunning cover jacket illustration by the famed artist Frederic Dorr Steele. This collected for the first time in book form Holmes short story pastiches and parodies by such authors as Mark Twain, O. Henry, Agatha Christie, Vincent Starrett and many others.

The Misadventures of Sherlock Holmes is the first non-Doyle Sherlockian anthology ever published, and it collects satires and pastiches published in the 50 year period from the 1890s to the 1940s. The book was involved in a copyright infringement with the Doyle Estate and as a result copies were recalled and destroyed. This almost ensured that an already very collectable and desirable Sherlockian book at the time, would today be quite scarce. It is scarce but copies do show up, with prices running from about $200 up to $1,000 for a very sharp copy in nice dust jacket. Signed or

The Seven-Per-Cent Solution

BEING A REPRINT FROM THE REMINISCENCES OF

John H. Watson, M.D. *as edited by* Nicholas Meyer

special associational copies can sell for thousands.

On an additional note, confusion sometimes exists on this book because that exact title was used for a recent Sherlockian anthology edited by Sabastian Wolfe in the UK. Collectors should note that the Wolfe edition is a totally different book from the Ellery Queen edition. First of all it is a mass-market paperback (Xanadu, UK, 1989). Both works are fine Sherlockian anthologies, only one or two stories appear in both. It was later reprinted in a trade paperback edition with dust jacket by Citadel Press, New York, 1991. More on these books in the following article.

In the meantime, the public demand for more Holmes stories was something that many publishers could not ignore. Nor could writers, most of whom are Holmes fans themselves, including Sir Arthur's son and a famed mystery writer. A decade later these two men joined forces to create a Sherlockian anthology of all *new* stories. This time it was an authorized edition. *The Exploits of Sherlock Holmes* (John Murray, London 1954; Random House, NY 1954) by Adrian Conan Doyle (Sir Arthur's son) and famed mystery author John Dickson Carr. They created a fine volume of new Holmes pastiche stories authorized by Doyle's son. This 12 story collection is based on unrecorded cases referred to by Watson in The Canon. The stories are all good, but not really great. Carr, a masterful writer, helped the younger Doyle in his efforts and the book is a prized collectable today.

Another early anthology of note was *The Science-Fictional Sherlock Holmes* edited by Robert C. Peterson (Council of Four, Denver, 1960). This 137 page collection of eight pastiches written by primarily science fiction writers who were also Holmes fans, includes: Poul Anderson, Gordon R. Dickson, Anthony Boucher, Mack Reynolds, August Derleth, and H. Beam Piper, with a nice five page Anthony Boucher introduction. This book is very scarce and much sought after, but many of the stories in it later appeared in the anthology *Sherlock Holmes Through Time and Space. The*

Science-Fiction Sherlock Holmes is available in either white or orange jackets (or perhaps both together). I'm not really sure. Really nice copies, when they show up, can sell for quite a bit of money. It is a most desireable book.

Another early Sherlockian pastiche was *Copper Beeches* by Arthur H. Lewis (Trident Press, 1971). While Sherlock does *not* appear, it concerns members of a scion society (fans) who use the Master's methods to solve a crime in the Holmes style.

The problem resulting from the publication of the Ellery Queen *Misadventures* and the fact that the Holmes stories were still under copyright at the time caused a hiatus on unauthorized Holmes pastiches for about 30 years. It wouldn't be until 1974 that a book would appear that would revolutionize the Holmes myth and the writing of pastiches (Sherlockian and non-Sherlockian) for decades to come.

II: The Seven-Per-Cent Formula

The Seven-Per-Cent Solution by Nicholas Meyer (US, Dutton, 1974; Hodder & Stroughton, UK, 1975) is a key book in the history of Sherlockian pastiche and key to this article. This was the first serious and highly successful Holmes pastiche and it also became a bestseller book and later a hit film. In this book, Holmes and Watson seek the aid of famed Vienna pyschiartrist Sigmund Freud and embark upon a new and fascinating case across Europe to save an actress from a German prince. It's a bit of a distaff Holmes because it focuses on his cocaine use overly much for some readers, but it is a well done tale.

By making use of the innovative device of incorporating actual historical persons of the era as part of his story, (Sigmund Freud, in this case), Meyer hit upon a unique formula, what I will call 'the formula.' This formula and variations of it, became the basis for the present successful pastiche novel. This important literary device would be used for the next quarter century in almost all pastiche fiction.

Meyer's 'formula' manifested itself in numerous ways in

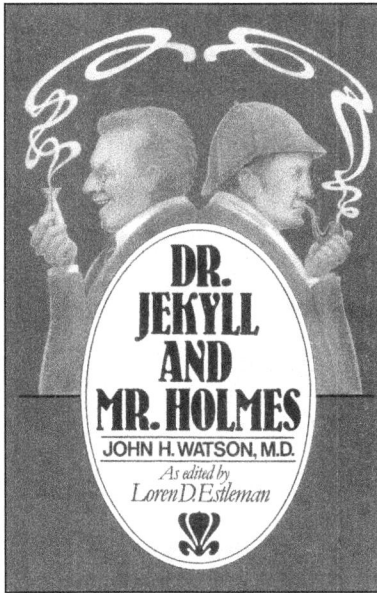

DR. JEKYLL AND MR. HOLMES

JOHN H. WATSON, M.D.
As edited by
Loren D. Estleman

Enter the Lion
A Posthumous Memoir of Mycroft Holmes

Edited by Michael P. Hodel and Sean M. Wright

most of the better and more innovative Sherlockian pastiches we'll look at in this article. There is an actual evolution to this 'formula' and it has various parts to it. In fact, there is a natural, chronological evolution here. In order of appearance, the formula dealt with: '*Alluded pastiches*,' stories based on Watson's alluded cases in the Canon. '*Team-ups*,' where Holmes and other famous actual persons (and even fictional persons) appear and work together (Theodore Roosevelt in *The Adventure of the Stalwart Companions*, Tarzan in *The Adventure of the Peerless Peer*, and even Karl Marx in one book). '*Spin-offs*,' where ancillary characters now have their own books, and later on their own series (Mrs. Hudson, Wiggins, Lestrade, Mycroft, and even Sherlock's son!). The last is the '*Sequels*,' pastiches written as sequels to the original Doyle stories (such as Hardwick's *The Revenge of the Hound* – a sequel to Doyle's *The Hound of the Baskervilles*.

Meyer tried to reprise his success two years later with a sequel of sorts, *The West End Horror* (Dutton, 1976), where Holmes tries to discover the perpetrator of bizarre murders

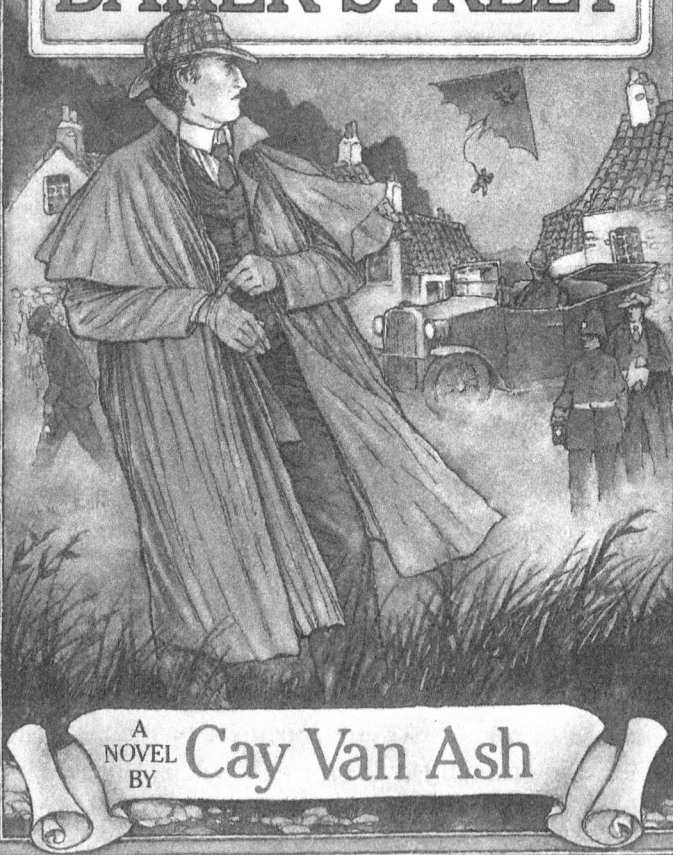

Ten Years Beyond
BAKER STREET

A NOVEL BY Cay Van Ash

in the London theatre district in 1895. Meyer has Bernard Shaw, Gilbert and Sullivan, Bram Stoker, Oscar Wilde and others appear in that one. It is a good read but did not have the impact or success of his first pastiche.

It would not be until 17 years later that Meyer would offer a Holmes pastiche for the third time with *The Canary Trainer* (Norton, 1993). This one tells the story of the Phantom of the Opera (pretty much from the Phantom's viewpoint). Meyer was never able to recoup the success of his first Holmes book, but all his work is well-written and I especially liked his first two books. I found *The Canary Trainer* a bit weak as a Holmes novel, actually more of a Phantom novel than a Holmes novel. In 2019 Meyer added a fourth Holmes pastiche to his list, *The Adventure of the Peculiar Protocols*.

However, Meyer's *The Seven-Per-Cent Solution* is a seminal work because it began the current pastiche process that has not ended to this day. While certainly not the earliest use of this formula, his book popularized the concept with readers, fans, publishers and writers. It was a concept that caught the imagination of a lot of people. Meyer's book began it all – and it has turned into a phenomena and today with some authors, a mini industry.

Once the copyright lapsed on the Holmes stories, the floodgates were open wide for imitation and pastiche. What Sherlockians enjoy now with so many pastiches is both wondrous and confusing. The desire to write a Sherlock Holmes story is something most writers and fans would like to do, and since Meyer had been so successful with his pastiche, many authors now wanted to try their own Holmes book. And they did with a variety of results! We'll take an overview of notable books and high points now and try to sort it out.

III: Pastiches of the 70s and 80s

At the same time that Meyer's *The Seven-Per-Cent Solution* was being published, science fiction writer Philip Jose

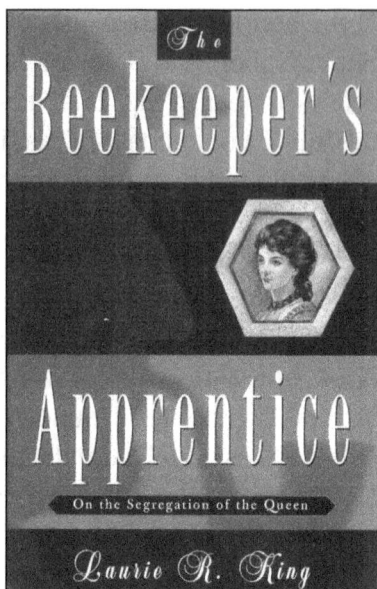

Farmer was busy writing a group of fun biographies of famous fictional characters, many from the grand old pulp magazines. One of note that appeared that same year was, *The Adventure of the Peerless Peer* (Aspen Press, 1974). This was a thin hardcover original from an obscure Colorado small press and is very scarce today in condition. In it Holmes goes to Africa and teams up on an adventure with no less a character than Edgar Rice Burroughs' famous jungle hero Tarzan! This World War I novel full of enemy Huns, zeppelins and famous air aces is a real blast. It was reprinted in a Dell paperback that is also scarce and collectable. Both are uncommon to find today but worth looking for.

Famed British mystery author Michael Dibdin began his crime writing career with a Holmes pastiche, that was also his first novel, *The Last Sherlock Holmes Story* (Jonathan Cape, UK, 1978; 1st US, Pantheon, 1978). This book is the first pastiche to deal with a famous crime that Doyle did *not* have Holmes investigate. But Dibdin does. He has Holmes called to investigate the Jack the Ripper murders in London's notorious East End that took place in 1888. Curiously, Doyle never had Holmes investigate the Ripper murders because he did not want to offend his reading public by sensationalizing and exploiting a series of fresh and ghastly murders that had left such an open sore in the British psyche of his era. However, that would not stop writers almost a century later from placing Holmes at the logical forefront of such an investigation. It seemed, after all, only natural. Dibdin's book is the first book on the subject (but certainly not the last).

However, there was one book on this subject even before Dibdin's. *Sherlock Holmes in A Study In Terror* (or in some editions, *A Study in Terror*) by Ellery Queen. The Lancer Books paperback original from 1966) is the actual first edition of this Holmes/Ripper novel. This Ellery Queen story, actually written by Paul W. Fairman, was an original paperback novel, a novelization of a film script for the film of the same name. The book follows the film quite closely, and both are excellent Holmes pastiches. *A Study in Terror* has many paperback reprints. It is actually an Ellery Queen story, but Queen is just the framing device to tell this early Holmes/Ripper tale.

Holmes vs. the Ripper yet again in one of the more recent single book pastiches, *The Whitechapel Horrors* by Edward B. Hanna (Carroll & Graf, 1992). A good Holmes novel and an interesting Jack the Ripper investigation.

One game that is fun for Sherlockians concerns the various allusions to unrecorded cases Doyle has Holmes or Watson mention throughout the Canon. Dropped into the various original stories, almost willy-nilly, these mysterious titles appear as intriguing and fascinating hints of further cases, kept secret for whatever reason. They have kept Sherlockians spinning and wondering for over a century. Naturally, writers of pastiche would seek to fill in these 'holes' in the Holmes mythos and answer our questions regarding these cases. I have even written one myself, *Sherlock Holmes in The Loss of the British Bark Sophy*

Anderson (Gryphon Books, pbo, 1994), concerning the goings on aboard that luckless ship, an underground cult, and bloody murder.

However, the most famous of all Watson's alluded cases has to be the strange case of the giant rat of Sumatra, as Holmes himself described it to Watson, "a story for which the world is not yet prepared". Now you can not get more intriguing than that!

The best book on the subject is *The Giant Rat of Sumatra* by Richard L. Boyer (Warner Books, pbo 1976; 1st hardcover, W.H. Allen, London 1977). The British edition is the first hardcover of Boyer's first book and sells for a high price. One of the best of all pastiche Holmes novels, it really captures the flavor and mood of the original Holmes stories and characters and tells a crackling good story. Highly collectable and sought-after, the paperback original is uncommon and can sell around $75, but that UK first hardcover is rare. There was also a US hardcover reprint published by Otto Penzler's The Mysterious Press, in their Armchair Detective Library in 1991.

Exit Sherlock Holmes by Robert Lee Hall (Scribners, 1977) chronicles Holmes last days. Old now, retired on the Sussex Downs and quietly keeping bees, or so you thought! This book takes place in 1930 — the actual year of Sir Arthur's death – and Holmes is called into action once again on another fascinating case. Hall's other book, *The King Edward Plot* (McGraw-Hill, 1980) contains the adventures of 'Wiggins,' one of Holmes 'Baker Street Irregulars.' Frederick Wigmore, a young actor now all grown up, solves a case of a plot against the King.

The Adventure of the Stalwart Companions by H. Paul Jeffers (Harper & Row, 1978) is a fun pastiche where Holmes teams-up on a case with the young, NYC Police Commissioner, Teddy Roosevelt. *'Bully, Holmes! Elementary, Teddy!'* The book works well because the Holmes and Teddy romp is a good match with two strong

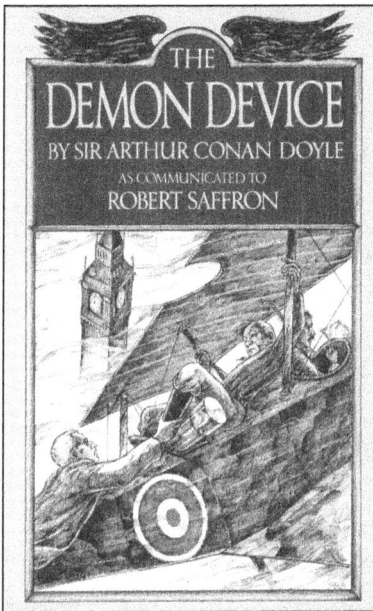

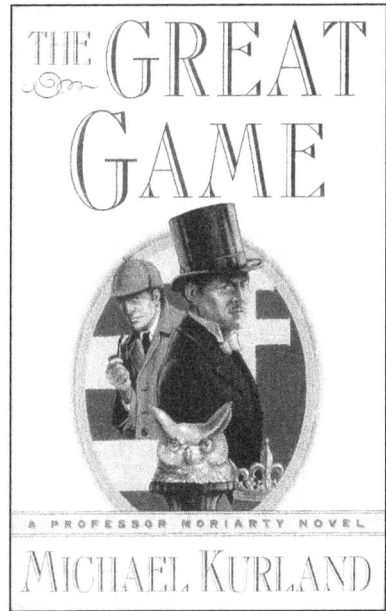

and interesting fun characters.

Since the pastiche 'formula' worked so well for Meyer and others so successfully, more writers began to get into the act and stretch the parameters of the Holmes pastiche. Crime and western author Loren D. Estleman contributed two fine novels that made good use of classic villains and extend the Holmes mythos into the horror field with Bram Stoker and Robert Louis Stevenson's fictional creations. These are *Sherlock Holmes Vs Dracula, or The Adventure of the Sanguinary Count* (Doubleday, 1978; New English Library, UK, 1978) and *Dr. Jekyll and Mr. Holmes* (Doubleday, 1979).

The Demon Device by Robert Saffron (Putnam, 1979) is another fine pastiche, but this time Doyle is the actual hero in a World War I adventure with flying spies and various enemies. It's an interesting premise that puts the author in the role of his character. While this fictional Doyle is no Sherlock Holmes, the book is a good adventure story and fun to read. Which is, after all, what these pastiches should be. A young Doyle would appear in a group of excellent novels by David Pirie, as a lead character. The books would eventually be adapted into a fascinating BBC TV series.

The Crucifer of Blood by Paul Giovanni (Doubleday, 1979, a slim 89 page first edition, book club edition) was based on the hit Broadway play. I saw the play when it ran on Broadway here in New York City and really enjoyed it, but I have never known about this book version until recently. This hardcover seems fairly scarce and seems to be the only edition of this play.

Sherlock Holmes in Dallas by Edmund Aubrey (Dodd, Mead, 1980) is exactly what you feared it might be, Holmes' investigation into the President Kennedy assassination in Dallas in 1963. This novel uses Holmes' methods to investigate this 'crime of the century,' and is an interesting look at the Kennedy assassination. It is also a pretty good Holmes novel if you can get past the rather outrageous premise of Holmes still alive and active in 1963!

In one book the master detective Holmes, and the master magician Houdini, meet in a team-up case. It's only natural, and more so, since Doyle and Houdini did know each other in real life. Doyle even tried to contact Houdini's ghost after the great magician died. *The Adventure of the Ectoplasmic Man* by Daniel Stashower (Morrow, 1985) is a fine novel that has these two icons working together. Stashower, a Sherlockian, and magician himself makes this Holmes/Houdini team-up work. Stashower has also written a fine Doyle biography as well.

Another team-up, this time between Holmes and Oscar Wilde occurs in *Sherlock Holmes and the Mysterious Friend of Oscar Wilde* by Russell A. Brown (St. Martins Press, 1988). Two mercurial minds at work!

With Professor Moriarity dead, and Col. Sebastian Moran ("the second most dangerous man in London") away in prison, you might think that really good Sherlockian villains may be hard to come by. However, these pastiche novels allow for some of the best villains to make an appearance in the Holmes mythos. Devotee of evil and Satanist Alistair

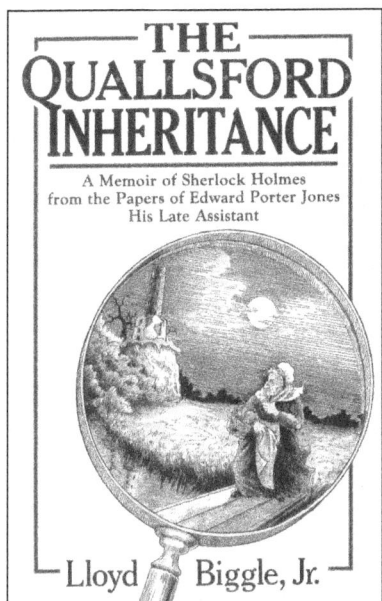

THE
QUALLSFORD
INHERITANCE

A Memoir of Sherlock Holmes
from the Papers of Edward Porter Jones
His Late Assistant

Lloyd Biggle, Jr.

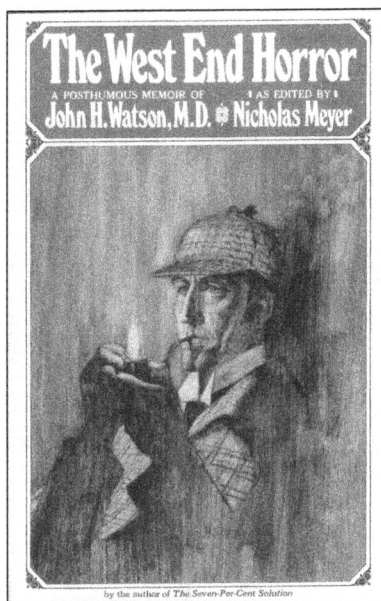

The West End Horror
A POSTHUMOUS MEMOIR OF   AS EDITED BY
John H. Watson, M.D. ❀ Nicholas Meyer

by the author of The Seven-Per-Cent Solution

Crowley appears as a heavy in *The Case of the Philosopher's Ring* by Randall Collins (Crown, 1978). This outstanding novel, incorporates much of the cult mysticism of the Victorian era and the many famous and infamous practitioners and philosophers who delved into the strange cults and dark forces of the era. It's certainly something different, and has very substantial 'points of interest' for many Sherlockians.

Eminent Sherlockian Michael Hardwick turned his hand to pastiche (he was already a fine Sherlockian scholar and author of many non-fiction studies of the Great Detective) with *The Revenge of the Hound* (Villard, 1987). This book is a fine sequel to the original Doyle novel, *The Hound of the Baskervilles*, and is highly thought of as one of the better pastiches ever written. Hardwick returned three years later with, *Prisoner of the Devil* (Proteus, 1990), a novel in which Holmes investigates the infamous Dreyfus Case in France.

One natural team-up would be Sherlock with his smarter brother Mycroft. They appear in *Enter The Lion* by Michael P. Hodel and Sean M. Wright (Hawthorn, 1979). Here the

THE NEW
SHERLOCK HOLMES NOVEL

THE
REVENGE
OF
THE
HOUND

Michael Hardwick

brothers work on a case that may very well overthrow the government of the United States and bring about a reconstituted Confederacy. The story is based on the notorious 'Trent Affair' during the American Civil War and extrapolates that event into the Victorian Era with Holmes and Mycroft working together – in their own way, of course!

One of the earliest Mycroft pastiches, *A Taste For Honey* (Vanguard Press, 1941) by H.F. Heard, was about a character called 'Mr. Mycroft.' He could be Sherlock Holmes in retirement and still taking cases, or Mycroft Holmes. Nevertheless, the H. F. Heard books are fun Sherlockian mysteries. The two sequels were, *Reply Paid* (Vanguard Press, 1942) and *The Notched Hairpin* (Vanguard Press, 1949). The first two books were reprinted in paperback and are easily available, the last was not and is scarce in the hardcover First. All three books were published together in hardcover in *The Amazing Mycroft Mysteries* by H.F. Heard (Vanguard Press, 1980), a first edition thus, that collected all three of these fine novels for the first time.

The first actual stand-alone Mycroft Holmes novel was *The Mycroft Memoranda* by Ray Walsh (St. Martins Press, 1984), yet another Holmes/Ripper novel. Though in truth, this book is less offensive to diehard Sherlockians than the earlier Dibdin book, and it offers many thrills, though in a somewhat distaff view also.

Mycroft Holmes would appear in many more novels and become the star of two series. The first series was by Glen Petrie. His first book was *The Dorking Gap Affair* (Bantam Press, UK, 1989). The sequel, *The Monstrous Regiment* (Bantam Press, UK, 1990) is about an unspeakable plot and death in the Tower of London.

Still yet another Mycroft series began in 1997 with, *Against The Brotherhood* by Quinn Fawcett (Tor Forge, 1997), in which Mycroft and his new secretary Patterson Guthrie embark on a tale full of assassinations, secret spymasters, cabals, double-agents and more. In the natural progression

of pastiche, rather than just a single novel, this book is the beginning of a series of books to star Mycroft Holmes, not Sherlock. The other two Fawcett books are *Embassy Row* (Forge, 1998) and his third Mycroft, *The Flying Scotsman* (Tor, 1999).

One writer who was one of the first to begin a pastiche series was Frank Thomas. Thomas many years before, as young Frankie Thomas, was the star of the early science fiction TV series, *Tom Corbett Space Cadet*. Years later, he grew up to be an avid Sherlockian. His books appeared as paperback original novels in the 1970s and early 1980s, most published by Pinnacle Books. However, he has one genuinely rare paperback original novel, *Sherlock Holmes and The Masquerade Murders* (Medallion Books, pbo, 1986; 1st hardcover, Otto Penzler Books, 1994). Here the paperback is more scarce than the Penzler reprint hardcover. The hardcover also uses the same cover art as the paperback but reverses it. In this novel Holmes and Watson try to solve a ghastly murder at a masquerade ball.

Holmes teams-up with fictional character Nayland Smith to

pursue the arch Asian villain Fu Manchu in *Ten Years Beyond Baker Street* by Cay Van Ash (Harper & Row, 1984). Van Ash, a Sax Rohmer scholar and biographer, does well in his first attempt to meld these two famous fictional characters into a good solid adventure.

We all know that Holmes and the Holmes myth are timeless, so it was only a matter of time before there was a Holmes pastiche that was an actual science fiction time travel novel. *Time For Sherlock Holmes* by David Dworkin (Dodd, Mead, 1983), features an immortal Holmes who has discovered the Elixir of Youth and Immortality! Now Holmes and Watson, who can live forever, investigate a case that takes place in the year 2170! This fine novel deals with H.G. Wells's time machine and Moriarity's master plan to use it to become absolute ruler of the future. A fun science fiction pastiche by a fine sf writer.

By this time, you can see that Sherlock Holmes seems to have met everyone in creation in these pastiches except maybe, Billy the Kid and King Kong. He even meets Karl Marx in one novel, *The Case of the Revolutionist's Daughter* by L. Feuer (Prometheus Books, 1983). I found this one rather dry and a bit too political of a Holmes tale by this Libertarian-oriented publisher.

Nicholas Utechin and Austin Mitchelson wrote two well received Holmes pastiches published in the US as paperback originals by Belmont Books in 1976. They're scarce today. *Sherlock Holmes and the Earthquake Machine* (Ian Henry, UK hardcover reprint, 1994) and *Sherlock Holmes and the Hellbirds* (Ian Henry, UK hardcover reprint, 1995; US title was just "Hellbirds"). The Ian Henry editions are British hardcover firsts.

Sherlock Holmes at the 1902 Fifth Test by Stanley Shaw (W.H. Allen, UK paperback original, 1985) is an interesting novel where Holmes assists England to defeat the Australians in a 1902 cricket match. Something different, Holmes with sports. Shaw also wrote *Sherlock Holmes Meets*

Annie Oakley (W.H. Allen, UK, 1986) where Holmes meets Annie Oakley when she was in England in 1887 with *Buffalo Bill's Wild West Show*.

Sherlock's son even makes an entrance onto the pastiche stage in *Rasputin's Revenge: The Further Startling Adventues of Auguste Lupa – Son of Holmes* by John T. Lescroart (Donald Fine, hardcover first, 1987) and he returns in *Rasputin's Revenge* (Donald Fine, hardcover first, 1987). These are fun books.

Sherlock Holmes Investigates The Murder in Euston Square by Ronald Pearsall (David & Charles, UK 1989) is a hardcover First in jacket. This one merges fact with fiction as Holmes investigates a real murder committed in 1877 but not discovered until 1879.

The Book of The Dead by Robert Richardson (St. Martin's Press, 1989), concerns the activities surrounding the disappearance of an unpublished Sherlock Holmes story that leads to murder in a country house. The text of the story is published in full in the book.

Science fiction author Llody Biggle, Jr., wrote two excellent Holmes pastiches reportedly from the papers of Edward Porter Jones, Holmes' late assistant. The first was *The Quallsford Inheritance* (St. Martins Press, hardcover, 1986). Later came, *The Glendower Conspiracy* (Council Oak, Tulsa, hardcover, 1990), in which Holmes and Porter discover a conspiracy that reaches across Britain. This is a small, paperback-sized hardcover original in jacket.

IV: Women Get in the Act, and the Pastiches of the 1990s

In the late 1980s and 1990s some excellent female authors, including L. B. Greenwood, Carole Nelson Douglas, June Thomson and Laurie R. King, among others turned their creative talents to hardcover Holmes pastiches. They created new series that add a special female focus to the pastiche with some excellent results. They are responsible for turning

The New Adventures of

SHERLOCK HOLMES

Original Stories by Eminent Mystery Writers

Edited by Martin Harry Greenberg and
Carol-Lynn Rössel Waugh

CENTENNIAL EDITION AUTHORIZED
BY THE CONAN DOYLE ESTATE

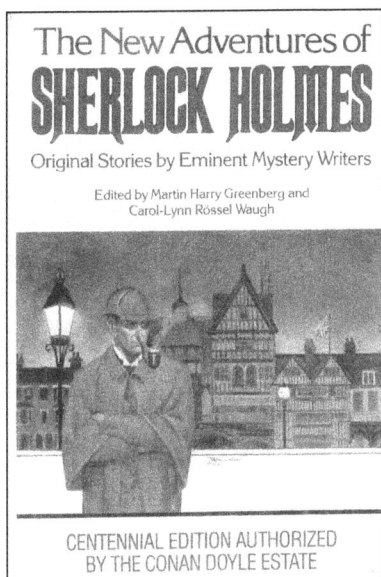

a new generation of men, and women, into Holmes fans, readers and collectors.

Canadian L. B. Greenwood's first novel, *Sherlock Holmes and the Case of the Raleigh Legacy* (Antheneum, US hardcover, 1987; Chivers Press, UK) was an excellent new Holmes pastiche novel. This was quickly followed by *Sherlock Holmes in the Case of Sabina Hall* (US hardcover, Simon & Schuster, 1988) and *Sherlock Holmes and the Thistle of Scotland* (US hardcover, Simon & Schuster, 1989).

Carole Nelson Douglas' four popular Irene Adler novels (also featuring Holmes) are very successful and well-written fun books. Her first was the best in the series, *Good Night, Mr. Holmes* (Tor, US hardcover, 1990). This was followed by *Good Morning, Irene* (Tor, US hardcover, 1991); *Irene At Large* (Tor, US hardcover, 1992), and *Irene's Last Waltz* (Tor Forge, US hardcover, 1994). All were later reprinted in paperback.

David Stuart Davies has written four fine Holmes pastiche novels to date. The first was *Sherlock Holmes and the Hentzau Affair* (Ian Henry, UK, 1991) based on Anthony

Hope's novel *The Prisoner of Zenda*. His next was, *The Tangled Skein* (Calabash Press, Canada, 1992) where Holmes has another encounter with Dracula. It also has a foreword by Peter Cushing. The third was, *The Scroll of the Dead* (Calabash Press, Canada, 1998). Davies also wrote, *The Shadow of The Rat* (Calabash Press, Canada, 1999). In this one an old acquaintance of Holmes and Watson appears with the plague, and begins an adventure that leads to a vast conspiracy.

Mark Frost made a bit of a splash with his first Sherlockian novel, *The List of 7* (US, Morrow hardcover, 1993; Hutchinson, UK hardcover, 1993 as *The List of Seven*) an incredible novel of sorcery, more conspiracy and world domination by a secret cabal. Moriarity cubed! The British edition of this may precede the US edition. Frost wrote a sequel that was just as good, *The Six Messiahs* (US, Morrow hardcover, 1995). The first book also came out in an interesting paperback original Advanced Reading Copy.

Another Sherlockian pastiche that travels the same ground that Nicholas Meyer investigated one year earlier in his *The Canary Trainer* is *The Angel of the Opera: Sherlock Holmes Meets the Phantom of the Opera* by Sam Siciliano (Penzler Books, US hardcover, 1994). I didn't especially like Meyers book *The Canary Trainer*, for me it was too much a Phantom book, but I think Siciliano did a better job of melding the two character and stories together into more of a true Holmes novel.

June Thomson is another writer, this time from England, who has taken on Doyle's legacy by producing new, and in most cases, very fine and enjoyable Holmes pastiche short fiction. Her "Secret" books came out in the UK from Constable and were reprinted in the US by Penzler Books. Her four pastiche collections include in order: *The Secret Files of Sherlock Holmes* (Constable, UK, 1990; Otto Penzler Books, 1990) containing eight original Holmes short stories, and *The Secret Chronicles of Sherlock Holmes* (Constable,

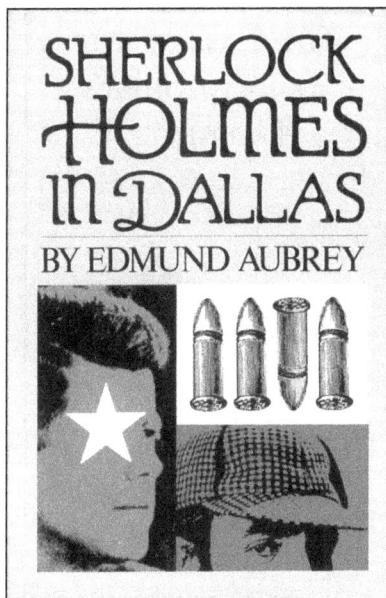

UK , 1992; Otto Penzler Books, 1994) with seven original stories including, "The Case of the Sumatran Rat!" Her third is *The Secret Journals of Sherlock Holmes* (Constable, UK , 1993) which contains seven pastiche tales. The fourth book is *The Secret Documents of Sherlock Holmes* (Constable, UK, 1997) which contains seven pastiches and includes the essay, "An Hypothesis Regarding the Real Identity of the King of Bohemia." Good non-fiction as well.

   Holmes and Watson: A Study in Friendship by June Thomson (Constable, UK hardcover, 1995) is a kind of pastiche biography of Holmes and Watson based on information given to us about them in The Canon. I don't know if there is a US reprint on this one.

   In 1990 British Holmes pasticher Clive Brooks self-published three hardcover Firsts that feature new short stories. These are scarce books and I believe they were published in 300 numbered signed limited editions. I do not know if they have been reprinted but they are worth searching for. They are *Sherlock Holmes Revisited: Volume One*, (Brook Books, 1990) which contains pastiches on the

THE CASE OF THE
REVOLUTIONIST'S
DAUGHTER

SHERLOCK HOLMES
MEETS KARL MARX

by
Lewis S. Feuer

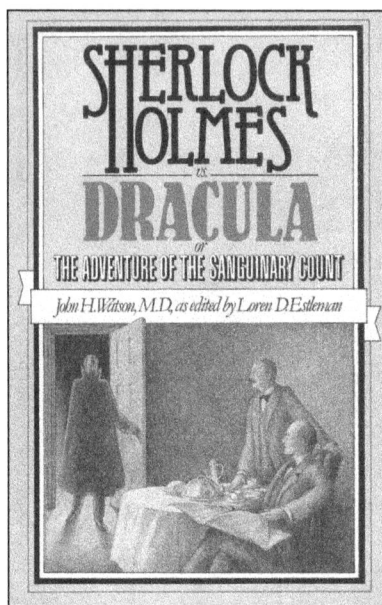

SHERLOCK
HOLMES
vs.

DRACULA
or
THE ADVENTURE OF THE SANGUINARY COUNT

John H.Watson, M.D., as edited by Loren D.Estleman

unpublished cases. *Sherlock Holmes Revisited: Volume Two* (Brook Books, 1990) with more pastiches based on unpublished cases. The third book is *The Memoirs of Professor Moriarity: Volume One* (Brook Books, 1990) which contains four pastiche stories of Moriarity's cases in which he found himself pitted against Holmes. Though this is listed as Volume One, there was no Volume Two.

One of the most recent and successful of Sherlockian pastiche authors has to be Laurie R. King. Her brilliant and scarce first novel *The Beekeeper's Apprentice* (St. Martins Press, US hardcover, 1994; Harper Collins, UK hardcover, 1996) is not only her first book but the first in her successful Mary Russell series. Mary Russell is a successful spin-off character, and she becomes Holmes wife and the two begin a new partnership solving criminal cases together. The books really capture the woman's delight in the stories and are responsible for bringing in many new female fans into the Holmes mythos, much as Douglas' Irene Adler books did. Other fine books in King's series include, in chronological order: *A Monstrous Regiment of Women* (St Martins, 1995;

Harper Collins, UK, 1997) ; *A Letter of Mary* (St. Martins, 1997; Harper Collins, UK, 1999); *The Moor (St. Martins, 1998)*; and the fifth Mary Russell novel, *O'Jerusalem* (US, Bantam harccover, 1999).

Other recent pastiche series of note are by British author Val Andrews, featuring Holmes and Watson in new cases. Most of these have appeared as trade paperback originals in the UK from Bresse Books. Breese has also published many paperback originals by John Hall, William Seil, J. M. Gregson and others, that unfortunately fall outside the scope of this article. However, some of the earlier Andrews novels have seen original publication as British hardcover Firsts by Ian Henry. Val Andrews began with *Sherlock Holmes and the Eminent Thespian* (Ian Henry, UK hardcover, 1988), a fun book that has Holmes and Watson investigating the theft of the Crown jewels, which leads them to the Lyceum Theatre where William Gillette is performing in the play 'Sherlock Holmes.' The next was *Sherlock Holmes and the Egyptian Hall Adventure* (Ian Henry, UK hardcover, 1989). There is also *Sherlock Holmes and the Brighton Pavilion Mystery* (Ian Henry, UK hardcover, 1989), where Holmes and Watson are involved in a classic locked-room mystery.

Larry Millett is another somewhat recent writer who has written three fine Sherlockian pastiche novels. His first was *Sherlock Holmes and the Red Demon* (US hardcover, Viking, 1996), with Holmes in Minnesota on a wild Ripper case that includes arson on the Great Northern Railway. Millett's other pastiches include, *Sherlock Holmes and the Ice Palace Murders* (US hardcover, Viking, 1998) and the third volume, *Sherlock Holmes and the Rune Stone Mystery* (US hardcover, Viking, 1999), where Holmes and Watson come to America on a case for King Oskar II of Sweden.

One of the longest-running spin-off series is M (eirion). J (ames). Trow's Sholto Lestrade series of 16 novels. The first appearance of Lestrade was in hardcover in the US from Stein & Day in 1985 in the novel, *The Supreme Adventure of*

Inspector Lestrade (reprinted as *Lestrade and The Ripper*). I believe this book is under-valued in the current market, but it is not too hard to find. There was also a mass-market paperback. All other books in this series were originally published in England as hardcover Firsts by Macmillan, and then by Constable. They were also reprinted as hardcover American Firsts by Regenry's Gateway Books, which as of this writing has just come out with number 10 in their series, *Lestrade and the Magpie*. Trow, a history teacher, combines his love of the Holmes pastiche with history in novels that highlight Lestrade. The books are witty and fun. Lestrade is the star here! Sweet revenge, for some.

In the Lestrade series there is some variation in the chronological order between the original UK editions to the editions of the present US publisher. The 16 book Lestrade series includes: *The Adventures of Inspector Lestrade* (Macmillan, UK 1985; Gateway, 1998), the author's first book and first Lestrade adventure. The British first is increasingly sought after and pricey.

Brigade: Further Adventures of Inspector Lestrade (Macmillan, UK, 1986; Gateway, 1998), the second book in the series, where Lestrade investigates the appearance of a lion in Cornwall and a series of suspicious deaths of old men who have died in their sleep.

Lestrade and the Ripper ([originally from Stein & Day, US, 1985 as *The Supreme Adventure of Inspector Lestrade*]; Macmillan, UK, 1988; Gateway, 1999) has Holmes and Lestrade both working on the Ripper case with Holmes getting in the Inspector's way! These are fun and witty books. All of Trow's Lestrade books are listed in the bibliography at the end of this article.

Throughout the 1990s, there have been quite a few authors who have written just one Holmes pastiche out of their main body of work. There have also been authors who have written a Holmes pastiche as their first book. Some of these books are:

The Seventh Bullet by Daniel D. Victor (US hardcover St Martins Press, 1992), not only a first edition pastiche but it is the author's first novel. In it Holmes and Watson have an American adventure.

A more recent book of interest is *A Samba for Sherlock* by acclaimed Brazilian author Jo Soares (Pantheon, 1st American edition translated from the Portugesse, 1997) in which Holmes takes on a case in South America and he and Watson appear in Rio.

The Secret Cases of Sherlock Holmes by Donald Thomas (Macmillan, UK 1997, Carroll & Graf, US, 1998) is an interesting group of Sherlockian short story pastiches, some involving characters like Jack the Ripper and Dr. Jekyll.

The Strange Case of Mrs. Hudson's Cat by Colin Bruce (Addison Wesley, UK hardcover, 1997) is a collection where Bruce recreates the atmosphere of the Holmes tales in 12 stories that feature Holmes and Watson explaining principles of physics. There is no US edition of this book as far as I know.

The Star of India by Carole Bugge (St. Martins Press, 1998), is a first novel by this talented author who went on to write many fine works.

The Surrogate Assassin by Christopher Leppek (Write Way Publishing, 1998), is also a first novel, and has Holmes and Watson investigate the Lincoln assassination.

The Problem of the Missing Miss by Toberta Rogon (St. Martins, 1998) is another First Edition, and the author's first book. This one has Lewis Carroll meeting with Doyle in a Victorian mystery.

Another interesting recent pastiche author is Barrie Roberts who has written five books so far all published as hardcover firsts in the UK by Constable. Roberts' first pastiche and first book is *Sherlock Holmes and the Railway Maniac* (Constable, UK, 1994). Others include, *Sherlock Holmes and the Man From Hell* (Constable, UK, 1997), and *Sherlock Holmes and the Royal Flush* (Constable, UK, 1998).

His most recent was, *Sherlock Holmes and the Harvest of Death* (Constable, UK, 1999). In this one Holmes and Watson travel to the west country of England to solve another strange case.

V: Some Recent Hardcover Anthologies

There have also been a recent early group of Sherlockian anthologies, short story collections by various authors trying their hand at a Holmes tale. The books are a mixed bag, obviously depending on the quality of the stories within. That quality can run from simply awful all the way up to supreme, fully capturing all the mood and flavor of the original Doyle tales. Most stories are well-done, professional work by writers who really care about the Holmes character and myth. These anthologies have proved popular over the years. They have appeared in hardcover and paperback, and there have been quite a number of paperback originals. I have already listed the early ones in the body of this article, but here are other hardcover Firsts:

Sherlock Holmes Through Time and Space edited by Isaac Asimov, Martin Harry Greenberg and Charles Waugh (Bluejay Books, 1984) an anthology of new and reprint Holmes tales that have a science fiction focus including work by many sf writers. A fine anthology that collects many of the classic pastiches from the rare *Science-Fictional Sherlock Holmes* in addition to new material.

The New Adventures of Sherlock Holmes, edited by Martin Harry Greenberg and Carol-Lynn Rossel Waugh (US hardcover, Carroll & Graf, 1987; Robinson, UK hardcover, 1999). This is a very successful anthology of pastiche short stories by eminent mystery writers. The Robinson reprint is an updated edition that includes four — at the time — new stories, by Stephen King, Bill Crider, Anne Perry and Daniel Stashower.

The Resurrected Holmes edited by Marvin Kaye (St. Martins, 1996) is a very fun and innovative idea, and it actually works in most of the stories. The premise here is original Holmes stories 'as if written' by other famous writers. So what you have is a Holmes story *as if* written by Mickey Spillane, or H.P. Lovecraft, or Ernest Hemingway. An interesting and fun premise and something truly original in the pastiche area. It also contains 'The Giant Rat of Sumatra' by Paula Volskey (as ascribed to H.P. Lovecraft!). Kaye would go on to become the fine editor of *Sherlock Holmes Mystery Magazine* and sadly passed away in 2021.

Holmes For The Holidays, edited by Martin H. Greenberg, Jon L. Lellenberg and Carol-Lynn Waugh (Berkley hc, 1996) is a collection of 14 original Holmes stories that celebrate and investigate the holiday season. One of the most successful of recent pastiche anthologies it spawned a sequel a few years later...

More Holmes For The Holidays edited by Jon L. Lellenberg and Carol-Lynn Waugh (Berkley, 1999) is a sequel of sorts to the earlier above book that was such a good seller over Christmas a few years back. This one has short stories by a host of famous authors including Anne Perry, Loren Estleman, Carolyn Wheat, Peter Lovesey, Tanith Lee and Barbara Paul.

And that about wraps things up.

I'm sure I've left out some favorites in this short article, that has after all, only scratched the surface of this rather extensive and ever-growing subject. A truly comprehensive listing would take many more pages than this book has to offer. I know that many more new Sherlock Holmes pastiches in novel and short story form are being written, perhaps even as you read this article. One thing can be said about Doyle's wonderful creation is that no one who has read all the original Sherlock Holmes stories, can resist the urge to read these pastiches. In their own way the authors here have done their best to keep the Holmes myth alive. They seek to entertain us all anew, once again taking us to that "Grand country of the mind where it is always 1895," or

thereabouts. And for the most part they have succeeded
admirably. Each pastiche offers something new, exciting, or
at least different, another view of Holmes. Or a new view of a
character in The Canon who grows in their own right to have
their own adventures, with Holmes, or without him. It's all
grand fun!

VI: Hardcover Pastiche Firsts: A Bibilography

The following list includes bibliographic data on all books
mentioned in the preceding article, alphabetically by author's
last name. I have listed all US Firsts, many UK Firsts, with
some key first hardcover editions and paperback originals.
Sherlockian books, of any type, are avidly collected.
Pastiches are just as avidly sought after. British Firsts are
scarce in condition because of low print runs. While demand
may be less in the US, supply is severely limited. Sherlockian
collectors avidly seek these for their collections. Many of
these books are very much desired, and hence valued highly
in the First Edition market, and the Sherlockian market. In
some cases the reverse holds true as Sherlockians
sometimes tend to over-value certain items. I have tried to
strike a mid-line between these two 'markets,' with a general
range of value. Prices are for Fine condition books in almost-
Fine jacket.

Andrews, Val, **Sherlock Holmes and the Eminent Thespian**, Ian
   Henry, London, 1988, $45-75.
—**Sherlock Holmes and the Egyptian Hall Adventure**, Ian Henry,
   London, 1989, $35-55.
—**Sherlock Holmes and the Brighton Pavilion Mystery**, Ian Henry,
   London, 1989, $35-55.

Ash, Cay Van, **Ten Years Beyond Baker Street**, Harper & Row, New
   York, 1984, $25- 45.

Asimov, Isaac, Martin Harry Greenberg and Charles Waugh, ed.,
   Sherlock Holmes Through Time and Space, Bluejay, New York,
   1984, $25-45.

Aubrey, Edmund, **Sherlock Holmes in Dallas**, Dodd, Mead, New York, 1980, $20-35.

Biggle, Lloyd, Jr., **The Quallsford Inheritance**, St Martins Press, New York, 1986, $20-35.
—**The Glendower Conspiracy**, Council Oak, Tulsa, 1990, $25-40.

Boucher, Anthony, **The Case of the Baker Street Irregulars**, Simon & Schuster, New York, 1940, $150-450.

Boyer, Richard L., **The Giant Rat of Sumatra**, Warner Books PBO, New York, 1976, $35-75; W.H. Allen, London, 1977, 1st hardcover and Boyer's first book, $200-450; 1st US hardcover, Armchair Detective Library, New York, 1991, $15-35.

Brooks, Clive, **Sherlock Holmes Revisited: Volume One**, Brook Books, London, 1990, $45-65.
—**Sherlock Holmes Revisited: Volume Two**, Brook Books, London, 1990, $65.
—**The Memoirs of Professor Moriarity: Volume One**, Brook Books, London, 1990, $75-125.

Brown, Russell A., **Sherlock Holmes and the Mysterious Friend of Oscar Wilde**, St. Martins Press, New York, 1988, $15-25.

Bruce, Colin, **The Strange Case of Mrs. Hudson's Cat**, Addison Wesley, London, 1997, $15-25.

Bugge, Carole, **Star of India**, St. Martins Press, New York, 1998, $20-30.

Collins, Randall, **The Case of the Philospher's Ring**, Crown, New York, 1978, $20-35.

Dibdin, Michael, **The Last Sherlock Holmes Story**, Jonathan Cape, London, 1978, author's 1st book, $175-400; Pantheon, New York, 1978, $45-65.

Davies, David Stuart, **Sherlock Holmes and the Hentzau Affair**, Ian Henry, London, 1991, $25-45.
—**The Tangled Skein**, Calabash Press, Canada, 1992, $60-65; reprinted, 1995, $15-25.
—**The Scroll of The Dead**, Calabash Press, Canada, 1998, $25-45.

—**The Shadow of the Rat**, Calabash Press, Canada, 1999, $25-30.

Douglas, Carole Nelson, **Good Night. Mr. Holmes**, Tor, New York, 1990, $25-65.
—**Good Morning, Irene**, Tor, New York, 1991, $15-35.
—**Irene At Large**, Tor, New York, 1992, $15-35.
—**Irene's Last Waltz**, Tor Forge, New York, 1994, $15-35.

Doyle, Adrian Conan, and John Dickson Carr, **The Exploits of Sherlock Holmes**, John Murray, London, 1954, $125-250.

Dworkin, David, **Time For Sherlock Holmes**, Dodd, Mead, New York, 1983, $15-35.

Estleman, Loren D., **Sherlock Holmes vs Dracula, or The Adventure of the Sanguinary Count**, Doubleday, New York, 1978, $15-35; New English Library, London, 1978, $35-75.
—**Dr. Jekyll and Mr. Holmes**, Doubleday, New York, 1979, $15-45.

Farmer, Philip Jose, **The Adventure of The Peerless Peer**, Aspen Press, Colorado, 1974, $90-175.

Fawcett, Quinn, **Against The Brotherhood**, Forge, New York, 1997, $20-35.
—**Embassy Row**, Forge, New York, 1998, $15-35.
—**The Flying Scotsman**, Forge, New York, 1999, $15-20.

Feuer, L., **The Case of the Revolutionist's Daughter**, Prometheus, New York, 1983, $15-29.

Frost, Mark, **The List of 7**, Morrow, New York, 1993, $35-50; Hutchinson, London, 1993, as **The List of Seven**, $30-55.
—**The Six Messiahs**, Morow, New York, 1995, $15-30.

Giovanni, Paul, **The Crucifer of Blood**, Doubleday, New York, 1979, $15-45.

Greenberg, Martin Harry and Carol-Lynn Rossell Waugh, ed., **The New Adventures of Sherlock Holmes**, Carroll & Graf, New York, 1987, $15-35.
—with Jon L. Lellenberg and Carol-Lynn Waugh, ed., **Holmes For the Holidays**, Berkley Books, Hardcover, New York, 1996, $15-35.

—with Jon L. Lellenberg and Carol-Lynn Waugh, ed., **More Holmes For the Holidays**, Berkley Books, New York, Hardcover, 1999, $15-25.

Greenwood, L.B., **Sherlock Holmes and the Case of the Raleigh Legacy**, Antheneum, New York, 1987, $30-35; Chivers Press, London, 1989?, $30-65.
—**Sherlock Holmes and the Case of Sabina Hall**, Simon & Schuster, New York, 1988, $15-35.
—**Sherlock Holmes and The Thistle of Scotland**, Simon & Schuster, New York, 1989, $15-35.

Hall, Robert Lee, **Exit Sherlock Holmes**, Scribners, New York, 1977, $20-35.
—**The King Edward Plot**, McGraw-Hill, New York, 1980, $15-30.

Hardwick, Michael**, The Revenge of the Hound**, Villard, New York, 1987, $20-35.
—**Prisoner of the Devil**, Proteus, New York, 1190, $15-30.

Hanna, Edward B., **The Whitechapel Horrors**, Carroll & Graf, New York, 1992, $20.

Heard, H.F., **A Taste For Honey**, Vanguard Press, New York, 1941, $75-175
—**Reply Paid**, Vanguard Press, New York, 1942, $85-175.
—**The Notched Hairpin**, Vanguard Press, New York, 1949, $60-175.
—**The Amazing Mycroft Mysteries**, Vanguard Press, New York, 1980, $20-45, collects the above three novels in one volume.

Hodel, Michael P. & Sean M. Wright, **Enter The Lion**, Hawthorn, New York, 1979, $15-35.

Jeffers, H. Paul, **The Adventure of the Stalwart Companions**, Harper & Row, New York, 1978, $15-25.

Kaye, Marvin, ed., **The Resurrected Holmes**, St. Martins Press, New York, 1996, $15-35.

King, Laurie, **The Beekeeper's Apprentice**, St. Martins Press, New York, 1994, $200-750, her first book and first in the Mary Russell series; Harper Collins, London, 1996, $95-225.
—**A Monstrous Regiment of Women**, St. Martins Press, New York,

1995, $40-45; Harper Collins, London, 1997, $20-45.
—**A Letter of Mary**, St. Martins Press, New York, 1997, $15-25; Harper
Collins, London, 1999, $20-35.
—**The Moor**, St. Martins Press, New York, 1998, $15-25.
—**O'Jerusalem**, Bantam Books, Hardcover, New York, $15-25.

Leppek, Christopher, **The Surrogate Assassin**, Write-Way Publishing,
Aurora, Co. 1998, $15-25.

Lescroart, John T., **Rasputin's Revenge: The Further Startling
Adventures of Auguete Lupa – Son of Holmes**, Donald Fine, New
York, 1987, $15-45.
—Rasputin's Revenge, Donald Fine, New York, 1987, $20-45.

Lewis, Arthur H., **Copper Beeches**, Trident Press, New York, 1971, $25-
45.

Lovisi, Gary, **Sherlock Holmes in the Loss of the British Bark Sophy
Anderson**, Gryphon, New York, PBO, 1994.

Meyer, Nicholas, **The Seven-Per-Cent Solution**, Dutton, New York,
1974, $35-125; Hodder & Stroughton, London, 1975, $40; Dutton ARC
trade pb $125.
—**The West End Horror**, Dutton, New York, 1976, $15-30.
—**The Canary Trainer**, Norton, New York, 1993, $15-25.

Millett, Larry, **Sherlock Holmes and the Red Demon**, Viking, New
York, 1996, $15-25.
—**Sherlock Holmes and the Ice Palace Murders**, Viking, New York,
1999, $15.
—**Sherlock Holmes and the Rune Stone Mystery**, Viking, New York,
1999,$15.

Pearsall, Ronald, **Sherlock Holmes Investigates the Murder in
Euston Square**, David & Charles, London, 1989, $20-35.

Peterson, Robert C., **The Science-Fictional Sherlock Holmes**, Council
of Four, Denver, 1960, $125-255.

Petrie, Glen, **The Dorking Gap Affair**, Bantam Press, London, 1989,
$25-45.
—**The Monstrous Regiment**, Bantam Press, London, 1990, $15-30.

Queen, Ellery, ed., **The Misadventures of Sherlock Holmes**, Little, Brown & Co., 1944, $400-$1,000.
—**A Study in Terror**, Lancer PBO, New York, 1966, $30-75.

Richardson, Robert, **The Book of The Dead**, St. Martins Press, New York, 1989, $15-45.

Roberts, Barrie, **Sherlock Holmes and the Railway Maniac**, Constable, London, 1994, $30-65.
—**Sherlock Holmes and the Man From Hell**, Constable, London, 1997, $35.
—**Sherlock Holmes and the Royal Flush**, Constable, London, 1998, $30-45.
—**Sherlock Holmes and the Harvest of Death**, Constable, London, 1999, $30.

Rogon, Toberta, **The Problem of the Missing Miss**, St. Martins Press, New York, 1998, $15-25.

Shaw, Stanley, **Sherlock Holmes at the 1902 Fifth Test**, W.H. Allen, London, 1985, $25-75.
—**Sherlock Holmes Meets Annie Oakley**, W.H. Allen, London, 1986, $30-55.

Siciliano, Sam, **The Angel of the Opera: Sherlock Holmes Meets the Phantom of the Opera**, Penzler Books, New York, 1994, $15-35.

Soares, Jo, **A Samba for Sherlock**, Pantheon, New York, 1995, 1st English language edition, $15-25.

Stashower, Daniel, **The Adventure of the Ectoplasmic Man**, Morrow, New York, 1985, $15-35.

Thomas, Donald, **The Secret Cases of Sherlock Holmes**, Macmillan, London, 1997, $15-30; Carroll & Graf, New York, 1998, $15-20.

Thomas, Frank, **Sherlock Holmes and the Masquerade Murders**, Medallion Books, PBO, Los Angeles, 1986, $75-125; Penzler Books, New York, 1st hardcover edition, 1994, $20-35.

Thomson, June, **The Secret Files of Sherlock Holmes**, Constable, London, 1990, $65-75; Penzler Books, New York, 1990, $15-20.

—**The Secret Chronicles of Sherlock Holmes**, Constable, London, 1992, $50-60; Penzler Books, New York, 1994, $15-20.
—**The Secret Journals of Sherlock Holmes**, Constable, London, 1993, $45-55.
—**Holmes and Watson: A Study in Friendship**, Constable, London, 1995, $60.
—**The Secret Documents of Sherlock Holmes**, Constable, London, 1997, $50.

Todd, Peter, **The Adventures of Herlock Sholmes**, Mysterious Press, New York, 1976; regular edition $15; signed edition $50.

Trow, M.J., **The Adventures of Inspector Lestrade**, Macmillan, London, 1985, $150-175; Gateway, Washington, 1998, $20-35.
—**Brigade: Further Adventures of Inspector Lestrade**, Macmillan, London, 1986, $75-100; Gateway, Washington, 1998, $15-30.
—**Lestrade and the Hallowed House**, Macmillan, London, 1987, $75-95; Gateway, Washington, 1999, $15-30.
—**Lestrade and the Leviathan**, Macmillan, London, 1987, $75-95; Gateway, Washington, 1999, $15-30.
—**Lestrade and the Ripper**, Stein & Day, New York, 1985, $25-55 **as The Supreme Adventure of Inspector Lestrade**; Macmillan, London, 1988, $55-95; Gateway, Washington, 1999, $15-30.
—**Lestrade and the Brother of Death**, Macmillan, London, 1988, $55-95; Gateway, Washington, 1999, $15-30.
—**Lestrade and the Guardian Angel**, Constable, London, 1990, $45-95; Gateway, Washington, 1999, $15-30.
—**Lestrade and the Deadly Game**, Constable, London, 1990, $45-75; Gateway, Washington, 1999, $15-30.
—**Lestrade and the Gift of the Prince**, Constable, London, 1991, $45-75; Gateway, Washington, US, 2000, $15-30.
—**Lestrade and the Magpie**, Constable, London, 1991, $65; Gateway, Washington, 2000, $15-20.
—**Lestrade and the Dead Man's Hand**, Constable, London, 1992, $75.
—**Lestrade and the Sign of Nine**, Constable, London, 1992, $75.
—**Lestrade and the Sawdust Ring**, Constable, London, 1993, $75.
—**Lestrade and the Mirror of Murder**, Constable, London, 1993, $75.
—**Lestrade and the Devil's Own**, Constable, London, 1996, $75.

Utechin, Nicholas, with Austin Mitchelson, **The Earthquake Machine**, Belmont Books, New York PBO, 1976, $25-45; Ian Henry, London, first hardcover and first British edition, 1994, as **Sherlock Holmes and**

The Earthquake Machine, $35-75.
—**Hellbirds**, Belmont Books, New York, PBO, 1976, $35-60; Ian Henry, London, first hardcover and first British edition, 1995 as **Sherlock Holmes and the Hellbirds**, $30-75.

Victor, Daniel D., **The Seventh Bullet**, St. Martins Press, New York, 1992, $20.

Walsh, Ray, **The Mycroft Memoranda**, St. Martins Press, New York, 1984, $15-30.

Wolfe, Sabastian, ed., **The Misadventures of Sherlock Holmes**, Xanadu, PBO, London 1989, $35-95; Citadel Press, TPB, New York, 1991, $15.

Sherlockian Misadventures

Sherlock's popularity knows no bounds. He's been written about by almost every writer of the 20th and 21st Centuries — in either fiction or non-fiction — in one guise or another. His popularity has achieved mythical status, and deservedly so, but there are other myths in the Sherlockian world and one of them is about his misadventures.

There have been literally hundreds of Holmes burlesques, parodies, and pastiches written; all misadventures which feature such thinly disguised Sherlockian characters as Thinlock Bones, Picklock Holmes, Shamrock Jolnes, Sherlaw Kombs, Holmlock Shears, and of course even, Solar Pons.

This cacophony of odd-sounding names existed for two reasons; the unparalleled popularity and love for the Great Detective, and the fact that Holmes stories and characters were under copyright by Sir Arthur Conan Doyle and his estate. Doyle died in 1930 — almost a hundred years ago — but it has been only in the last few decades that eventually all of his tales have fallen into the public domain. Hence the slew of recent pastiches using the actual Holmes character. In the past, if a writer wanted to write a Holmes story, or use a Sherlockian character (or even a story that featured Holmes himself), he had to do so under one of the various Sherlockian guises.

There was a lot of material published in this manner, and much of it was quite good — most of it appearing in the earlier part of the 20th Century in now obscure and often pricey magazines. It's always an event when a new book appears on the market that collects such tales for us

The
MISADVENTURES
of
SHERLOCK
HOLMES

STORIES ABOUT SHERLOCK HOLMES
written by MARK TWAIN, O. HENRY,
BRET HARTE, AGATHA CHRISTIE,
STEPHEN LEACOCK, CAROLYN WELLS,
VINCENT STARRETT, and many others.

EDITED BY
ELLERY QUEEN

between its covers.

Such a volume is *The Misadventures of Sherlock Holmes*, edited by Sebastian Wolfe, and published as a first edition paperback from Xanadu Books in England in 1989 (ISBN 1854800094, L3.99m 249pp). The unaccredited cover art shows Holmes lighting his pipe, a woman in the background, and is quite effective.

This book states proudly on the back cover that it is "A Paperback Original — Never Before Published". Actually, it is *not* a paperback original, because all the stories in the book, except one, have had previous print publication. However, the book is a true first edition in paperback and has never before appeared — even though that exact title has been used on another classic Sherlockian anthology. Confused? Well, so was I, until I compared the two books and their contents. Here's what I discovered.

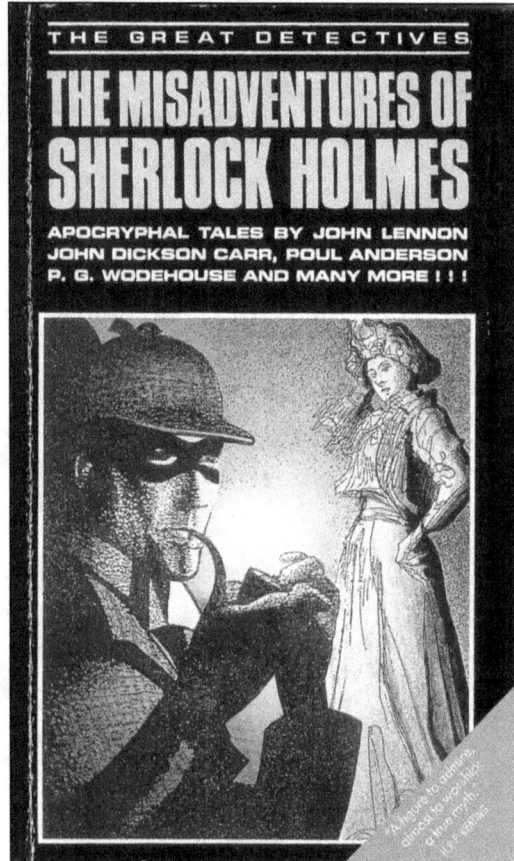

The Xanadu paperback edition first appeared in 1989. Xanadu, back then, was a new British paperback publisher and had just begun their "Great Detective Series", with this book. Well, what Great Detective series would be worth its salt without a volume of stories about the greatest detective of them all — Sherlock Holmes!

So a Holmes book was needed, but it could not be one of the canonical volumes by Doyle — after all, these had been printed and reprinted and were easily available. The canonical tales by Doyle were also known inside and out by any Sherlockains worth their salt. What Xanadu needed was something new, something no other publisher had done yet, so Wolfe put together this anthology of Sherlockain short stories written by other writers.

The Misadventures of Sherlock Holmes contains 14 gems that will bring a sparkle to any Sherlockian's eyes. They are, in order of appearance: "The Martian Crown Jewels" by Poul Anderson; "From The Diary of Sherlock Holmes" by Maurice Baring; "The Anomaly of The Empty Man" by Anthony Boucher; "The Adventure of The Paradol Chamber" by John Dickson Carr; "The Adventure of the Conk-Singleton Papers" by John Dickson Carr; "The Adventure of The Snitch in Time" by August Derleth and Mack Reynolds; "The Adventure of the Dog In The Knight" by Robert L. Fish; "The Adventure of the Three Madmen" by Philip Jose Farmer; "Mr. Montalba, Obsequist" by H.F. Heard; "A Trifling Affair" by H.R.F. Keating; "The Great Detective" by Stephen Leacock; "The Singularge Experience of Miss Anne Duffield" by John Lennon [of *Beatles* fame!]; "The Affair of The Midnight Midget" by Ardath Mayhar; and "From A Detective's Notebook" by P.G. Wodehouse. It is a most impressive line-up, great stories by truly great writers! There is also a two-page introduction by Wolfe and two pages of "Acknowledgements" listing prior publication of these stories. Many of these tales never appeared in Britain (which is key because this is a British paperback with no U.S. publication that I know of), and there is one story here that has never appeared in book form anywhere.

There's a lot of gold to mine here for the devoted Sherlockai. Many of the titles are plays on Doyle's original

tales, or attempts to fill in the gaps in Holmes' career. The
John Lennon piece is an interesting inclusion by the former
Beatle; the Farmer, Derleth/Reynolds, Boucher and
Anderson pieces are all finely science fiction-inspired and
offer new looks at the Holmes Mythos. This book is a solid
collection with a lot of good material — but that title really
got me thinking as soon as I saw it on this book. At first, I
wondered if this could be, in fact, a reprint of the rare 1944
hardcover volume with the same title? The fact that this is a
British paperback made the book a little more difficult to
obtain, but I did track down a copy in my own version of a
literary detective case.

As many Sherlockian's know, way back in 1944 there was
another book published with the title, *The Misadventures of
Sherlock Holmes*. That book has a most curious history. We
will take a look at it now.

That original volume was a first edition hardcover
anthology published in 1944 by Little, Brown and Company
(363 pages, original price $2.50), and was edited by famed
crime author Ellery Queen — or at least credited to him. It
contains a wealth of Sherlockian parodies and pastiches and
has never been reprinted. The contents are in four parts, and
are, in order of appearance: **PART I by Detective Story
Writers:** 1892, "The Great Pegram Mystery" by Robert Barr;
1907, "Holmlock Shears Arrives Too Late" by Maurice
Leblanc; 1915, "The Adventure of the Clothes-Line" by
Carolyn Wells; 1920, "The Unique Hamlet" by Vincent
Starrett; 1925, "Holmes And The Dasher" by Anthony
Berkley; 1929, "The Case of The Missing Land" by Agatha
Christie; 1942, "The Adventure of the Illustrious Impostor: by
Anthony Boucher; 1943, "The Disappearance of Mr. James
Phillimore" by Ellery Queen; 1943, "The Adventure of the
Remarkable Worm" by Stuart Palmer; **PART II by Famous
Literary Figures:** 1893, "The Adventure of the Two
Collaborators" by Sir James M. Barrie; 1902, "A Double-
Barreled Detective Story" by Mark Twain; 1902, "The Stolen

Cigar Case" by Brett Harte; 1911, "The Adventure of
Shamrock Jolnes" by O. Henry; **PART III by Humorists:**
1893, "The Umbrosa Burglary" by R.C. Lehmann; 1897, "The
Stranger Unravels A Mystery" by John Kendrick Bangs; 1911,
"Maddened By Mystery, or, The Defective Detective" by
Stephen Leacock; 1916, "An Irreducible Detective Story" by
Stephen Leacock. **PART IV by Devotees and Others:** 1894,
"The Adventure of the Table Foot" by Zero (Allan Ramsay);
1894, "The Sign of The '400'" by R.K. Munkittrick; 1907, "Our
Mr. Smith" by Oswald Crawford; 1920, "The Footprints on
The Ceiling" by Jules Castier; 1927, "The End of Sherlock
Holmes" by A.E.P.; 1928, "The Adventure of The Norcross
Riddle" by August Derleth; 1929, "The Mary Queen of Scots
Jewel" by William O. Fuller; 1932, "His Last Scrape: Or
Holmes, Sweet Holmes!" by Rachel Ferguson; 1933, "The
Adventure of the Murdered Art Editor" by Frederic Dorr
Steele; 1933, "The Canterbury Cathedral Murder" by Frederic
Arnold Kummer and Basil Mitchell; 1934, "The Case of The
Missing Patriarchs" by Logan Clendening, M.D.; 1935, "The
Case of The Diabolical Plot" by Richard Mallett; 1936,
"Christmas Eve" by S.C. Roberts; and from 1941, "The Man
Who Was Not Dead" by Manly Wade Wellman.

There are also two pages of "Acknowledgements", a five
page "Biography", and a one page index, all topped off by a
14-page "Introduction" by editor, Ellery Queen. There is also
an interesting editor's preamble to each story. This book was
one of four Ellery Queen anthologies published in hardcover
by Little, Brown & Company. It contained 33 short stories —
only *one* of which was reprinted in the later Wolfe edition!
That story was "Maddened By Mystery: or, The Defective
Detective" by Stephen Leacock — it appears in the Wolfe
anthology under the title of "The Great Detective" by
Stephen Leacock. Not a bad track record, only one
overlapping story between these two books, with a total of46
separate fine Sherlockian tales between them.

Well, it turned out that the Doyle estate did not approve of

the Queen edition at all, and by using the name of Sherlock
Holmes in the title, the publishers had strayed
(unintentionally, I'm sure) into the area of copyright
infringement. This was, after all, way back in 1944. So the
long and the short of it was that the Queen anthology was
recalled by Little, Brown & Company and all copies were
destroyed. But not all were destroyed — as some were sold!

Today, that Ellery Queen Holmes anthology is an
uncommon and much sought-after volume. I remember
seeing some nice condition copies selling for between $300
and $500 at Bouchercon — the World Mystery Convention
— in 1989. More recently, nice copies in dust jacket, can go
from $300 up to $1,000. The book has never been reprinted
and obviously never will be reprinted, but it is a cornerstone
of any true Sherlock Holmes collection. After the original
magazine appearances of the Doyle Holmes stories, or the
canonical volumes themselves in first editions, this book is
surely one you'll want to own.

The introduction by Ellery Queen is fascinating reading in
its own right and the book features a stunning black-
bordered dust jacket showing Holmes in profile, puffing
thoughtfully on his pipe. The jacket art is by the great
Frederic Dorr Steele, one of the best Holmes illustrators of
all time.

When I heard about the newer Wolfe edition I knew I had
to get a copy and see just what we had. Was it the same
book? Were the stories the same? Well, now you and I know
the truth. What we have here in the British Xanadu
paperback edited by Wolfe is a sort of modern equivalent of
that recalled 1944 Ellery Queen anthology — but they are
NOT the same book.

Wolfe, himself, writes in his introduction to the Xanadu
paperback: "Finally I should perhaps explain that only as the
contents of this book were being finalized, when it was too
late to make changes, did I learn of the existence of an
earlier volume with the same title, edited by Ellery Queen in

1944. I have not been able to locate a copy of that book — it was suppressed, I gather, by the Conan Doyle estate — so any resemblances between that *Misadventures* and this one are necessarily coincidental."

The Xanadu paperback can be ordered from rare book dealers who specialize in British out-of-print books or Sherlockania. You might also find a copy on ABE Books or Ebay, or some other online book site, but it might take some hard looking.

Both of these books may prove rather difficult to find in their original editions. The Queen book without a dust jacket, or a worn copy, may still cost you about $100 or more. I expect the Xanadu paperback sold quickly. I do not believe that Xanadu is still in business. To my knowledge this book has not been printed in the U.S., but I seem to recall seeing a reprint of it by another publisher years ago, perhaps in the U.K.?

Needless to say, both of these fine books would be a worthy addition to any Sherlock collection, and may be essential reading for any serious Holmes fan or collector.

So there you have it, two interesting books to search for if you do not already have copies. Two books with the *same* title, on the *same* topic, but *not* the same at all. And so it appears, dear collector, once again, *the game's afoot!*

Tauchnitz Books:
The Early Doyle Paperbacks

Introduction:

The collecting of Sherlock Holmes material is an endless quest for many of us die-heard fans, but it can also be fascinating, fun, educational, and always adventuresome. As Holmes was fond of saying, "the game is afoot!" so once again we go on a bibliographical search and discovery for some obscure and very early Holmes and Doyle paperback books.

One of the most interesting group of books to collect and one of the most difficult to obtain for the true Sherlockian completist, are the scarce Tauchnitz editions of Sherlock Holmes and the non-Sherlockian works by Sir Arthur Conan Doyle, published in this series in the later part of the 19th Century and the earlier part of the 20th Century. Almost all of which are now over one hundred years old!

There are ten Sherlock Holmes books in the series (three are two-volume sets), as well as there being 32 other Doyle editions that are not Sherlockain in content (seven of these are also in 2-volume sets as well). This is a fascinating series to collect but the books are hard to find — especially in nice condition — and completing the entire Doyle set is almost impossible to accomplish. My own set of these books is not complete and I have been collecting them for 30 years, and I do not know of anyone who has a complete Doyle set. Perhaps, fan and collector extraordinaire, John Bennett Shaw may have when he was alive but I never viewed his magnificent collection. With a total of 42 separate books by Doyle in this Tauchnitz series, it can be a very tough search to find any of them at all these days.

TAUCHNITZ EDITION
COLLECTION OF BRITISH AND AMERICAN AUTHORS
VOL. 2812

A STUDY IN SCARLET

BY

A. CONAN DOYLE

IN ONE VOLUME

LEIPZIG: BERNHARD TAUCHNITZ
PARIS: LIBRAIRIE HENRI GAULON, 39, RUE MADAME

A complete catalogue of the Tauchnitz Edition, with a list of the latest
additions on page 1, is attached to this volume

Not to be introduced into the British Empire

TAUCHNITZ EDITION
COLLECTION OF BRITISH AND AMERICAN AUTHORS
VOL. 4790

THE CASE-BOOK OF
SHERLOCK HOLMES

BY

A. CONAN DOYLE

LEIPZIG: BERNHARD TAUCHNITZ

Not to be introduced into the British Empire or U.S.A.

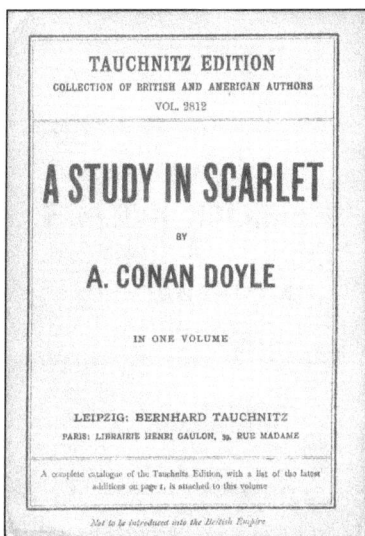

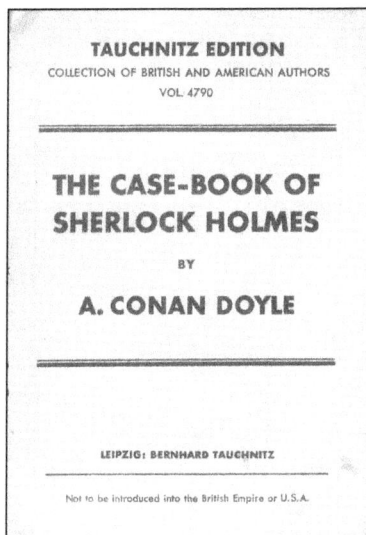

Publishing History:

Tauchnitz Books were probably the original English-language, mass-market paperback. The series is old; it began in the 19th Century in 1841 in Leipzig, Germany. It was begun by Christian Bernhard (later Baron) Tauchnitz.

These are elegant and classy volumes that denote a certain European charm and respect for quality literature. These are *not* pulp at all! In fact, they may often appear as rather bland to most modern paperback readers and collectors, who are used to the colorful (and sometimes lurid) illustrated cover art used on vintage era (1939-1969) paperbacks. However, these books in nice condition, to true collectors and readers, are beautiful and elegant — very desirable. To have a scarce Tauchnitz edition of a favorite classic book or author is a prize in any book collection and an edition any collector worth his salt will surely cherish.

Tauchnitz editions or "Tauchnitz English-language Continental Editions" were a series of paperbound books with non-illustrative covers, but they did have slight format and design changes on the covers over the years. All the books were printed in English and editions feature the best

TAUCHNITZ EDITION
COLLECTION OF BRITISH AND AMERICAN AUTHORS
VOL. 3571

THE HOUND
OF THE BASKERVILLES

BY

A. CONAN DOYLE

IN ONE VOLUME

LEIPZIG: BERNHARD TAUCHNITZ
PARIS: LIBRAIRIE HENRI GAULON, 39, RUE MADAME

The Copyright of this Collection is purchased for Continental Circulation only, and the volumes may therefore not be introduced into Great Britain or her Colonies.

A complete catalogue of the Tauchnitz Edition, with a list of the latest additions on page 1, is attached to this volume.

TAUCHNITZ EDITION
COLLECTION OF BRITISH AND AMERICAN AUTHORS
VOL. 2972

THE MEMOIRS OF
SHERLOCK HOLMES

BY

A. CONAN DOYLE

In Two Volumes. — Vol. 1

LEIPZIG: BERNHARD TAUCHNITZ
PARIS: LIBRAIRIE GAULON & FILS, 39, RUE MADAME

Not to be introduced into the British Empire and U.S.A.

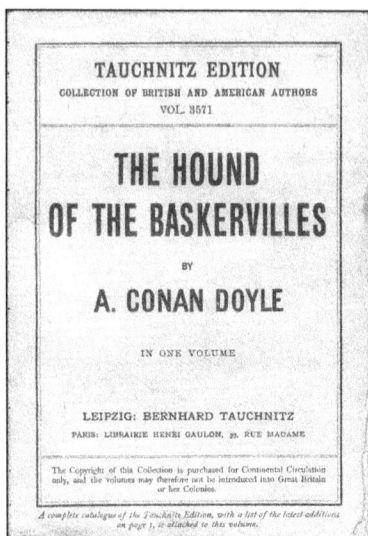

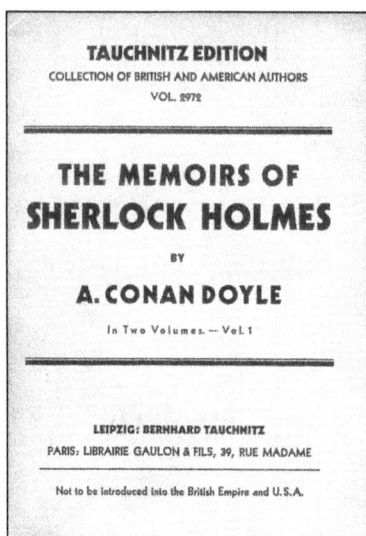

work of British and American authors. They were for sale and distribution only on the European continent and in at least 55 countries around the world.. They were *not* for distribution in English-speaking countries (hence the admission on each book that they were *not* to be distributed or sold in the UK or USA). This was the result of a gentleman's agreement among publishers that held firm for over 100 years, stipulating that the books were "Not to be introduced into the British Empire or U.S.A."

Tauchnitz was a class operation. They paid all their writers, even though this was before any international copyright agreements and hence, they were not legally forced to pay anyone for the books they published. Even the living authors — but they did! In an era of rampant book piracy and little respect for author rights, this was novel and very much appreciated. The Baron wanted to keep a good relationship with his authors and respected them. And they respected him.

Tauchnitz Books were roughly the size of American Handi-Books, about 4.5" x 1.5" in size, but about twice the thickness, being about ½" to 5.8" thick. All books were numbered on the cover and spine. They had thin paper covers that do not hold up very well, and cheap paper guts with edges usually (especially in the early days) uncut or untrimmed. For instance, Tauchnitz Book #1000 was *The Bible*, published in 1869. There were, by 1943, an incredible 5,370 volumes in the entire series, representing 783 English and American authors!

Tauchnitz Books and Authors:

The first Tauchnitz Book was published in 1841, and was Bulwer-Lytton's *Pelham*. Their second book was by a guy named Charles Dickens! Tauchnitz published work by all the greats of their day, such as Dickens, Disraeli, Thackeray, and A. Conan Doyle. They also published Zane Grey, Jack London, Edgar Allen Poe, Mark Twain, Robert Louis Stevenson (all their classic titles), and other collectable authors such as P.G. Wodehouse, Rudyard Kipling, H. Rider Haggard, H.G. Welles, Edgar Wallace, C.K. Chesterton, and as far as I can tell at least six books by Edgar Rice Burroughs, including *Jungle Tales of Tarzan*. New books appeared every week!

Most of the books in the series by Conan Doyle appeared in the later 3,000 number range, and were published originally in the series from about 1895 to 1920. Some were later. The earliest Doyle book Tauchnitz published and the first Sherlock Holmes book in their series was *The Sign of Four* (#2698, which must be from about 1895). The last was *The Casebook of Sherlock Holmes* (#4790) from about 1927.

The Non-Sherlockian Doyle:

Of the non-Sherlockian books in the Tauchnitz series, we have a good selection of Doyle's work in all genres; his adventure, historical, and ghostly suspense. There were two war books. There were also many uncommon volumes and collections of short stories.

The White Company (#2787 and 2788) was one of Doyle's

TAUCHNITZ EDITION
COLLECTION OF BRITISH AND AMERICAN AUTHORS
VOL. 4905

THE MARACOT DEEP

BY

A. CONAN DOYLE

IN ONE VOLUME

LEIPZIG: BERNHARD TAUCHNITZ
PARIS: LIBRAIRIE GAULON & FILS, 39, RUE MADAME

A complete catalogue of the Tauchnitz Edition, with a list of the latest
additions on page 1, is attached to this volume

Not to be introduced into the British Empire

TAUCHNITZ EDITION
COLLECTION OF BRITISH AND AMERICAN AUTHORS
VOL. 4008

THROUGH
THE MAGIC DOOR

BY

A. CONAN DOYLE

IN ONE VOLUME

LEIPZIG: BERNHARD TAUCHNITZ
PARIS: LIBRAIRIE HENRI GAULON, 39, RUE MADAME

The Copyright of this Collection is purchased for Continental Circulation
only, and the volumes may therefore not be introduced into Great Britain
or her Colonies.

A complete catalogue of the Tauchnitz Edition, with a list of the latest additions
on page 1, is attached to this volume.

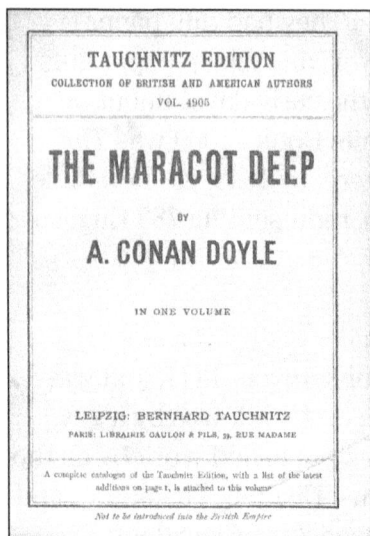

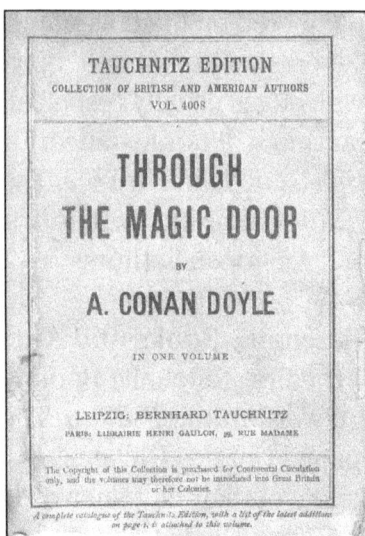

best historical novels; *The Lost World* (#4379) from about
1922, was the first Professor Challenger book in the series
and the first paperback printing of this classic novel. It's
sequel, or sorts, *The Poison Belt* (#4452) appeared a few
years later.

There isn't a lot written about the Tauchnitz Books as far as
I can find. Since they were published so long ago and not
sold in America or the U.K., access was limited to these
books for most collectors and readers. Only people traveling
to the continent of Europe and looking for English-language
material to read while on vacation (or "holiday"), actually
bought these books — or were able to purchase them. Some
of these travelers brought the books back home with them
to America or the U.K. Nevertheless, there are not many
editions that turn up here in the United States, so research is
difficult. Dating the publication of the books can be very
difficult as well, since while some books clearly list dates,
others do not and some facts seem to contradict each other.
There were also probably later reprints of earlier editions,
probably with the same book number. That can make things
even more confusing.

Values:

It may not be easy to find these books but they offer an interesting search and the Doyle books in the series are all prime collectables. Any of the Sherlock Holmes books in the series in nice condition can go for about $100, while the non-Sherlockain Doyle editions in like condition can probably fetch about $50-75, depending on title. The exception here could be *The Lost World* (#4370) which would probably go for at least $100 in really nice condition. All these books are scarce in clean collectable condition, which paperback book collectors term as VG, VG+, or if at all possible — Near Fine.

For Further Reading:

I believe the best source for further serious information on this publisher may be the book, *Tauchnitz International Editions In English 1841-1955: A Bibliographical History* by William B. Todd and Ann Bowden (1,078 pages, 90 illustrations, $75 original price), available from The Bibliographical Society of America. While I have not had the opportunity to examine this book I am assured it is a cornerstone volume on this important publisher and well worth the purchase price for any serious Tauchnitz collector. It is probably out of print today, and may take some searching for itself.

The List:

What follows is a list of all Tauchnitz Books by Sir Author Conan Doyle that I could find. I have listed the Sherlock Holmes books first, then the non-Holmes editions.

I hope you enjoy this article and list and that it will whet your appetite for more. I've listed as much information as I could find from books in my own collection as well as information listed in the back of many Tauchnitz Books by Doyle and many other authors spanning the years from 1900 to 1940. I also had access to collections and books by fellow collectors and Internet research helped as well.

Tauchnitz Sherlock Holmes Editions:
7 books published in 10 separate editions.
The Sign of Four, #2698, from about 1895.
A Study In Scarlet, #2812.
The Adventures of Sherlock Holmes, 2 volumes, #2896 and 2897.
The Memoirs of Sherlock Holmes, 2 volumes, #2872 and 2973.
The Hound of The Baskervilles, #3571.
The Return of Sherlock Holmes, 2 volumes, #3796 and 3797.
The Casebook of Sherlock Holmes, #4790, from about 1927.

Tauchnitz Non-Sherlockian Editions:
25 books published in 32 separate editions.
Micah Clarke, 2 volumes, #2740 and 21741.
The Captain of The Pole Star and Other Tales, #2762.
The White Company, 2 volumes, #2787 and 2788.
The Great Shadow and Beyond The City, #2886.
The Refugees, 2 volumes, #2919 and 2920, July, 1893.
Round The Red Lamp, #3040.
The Exploits of Brigadier Gerard, #3122.
Uncle Bernac, #3222.
The Tragedy of Korosko, #3262.
A Duet, #3354.
The Green Flag, Etc., #3425.
The Adventures of Gerard, #3700.
The Firm of Gridlestone, 2 volumes, #?
Through The Magic Door, #4008, about 1926.
Round The Fire Stories, #4007.
The Mystery of Cloomber, #4138.
The Last Galley, #4260.
The Lost World, #4370.
The Poison Belt, #4452.
The Land of Mist, #4728.
The Stark Munro Letters, #?
Rodney Stone, 2 volumes, #?

The Great Boer War, 2 volumes, #?
The War in South Africa, #?
Sir Nigel, 2 volumes, #?

Forever Holmes:
The Penzler Books'
"Sherlock Holmes Library"

O tto Penzler is a man whose name is well-known in the
annals of Mysterydom. He is the founder and owner of
The Mysterious Bookshop, a wonderful book-lovers
paradise in New York City; publisher of the late and
lamented *The Armchair Detective* magazine; devoted
mystery and crime fiction collector and dedicated
Sherlockian. Penzler is a man who wears many hats. One of
his most interesting talents is that of editor and publisher. In
1993, Penzler started a new paperback line bearing his name,
Otto Penzler Books (published and distributed by Macmillan
Books in New York City), and the centerpiece of this new
line was his wonderful "Sherlock Holmes Library". An
important Sherlockian book event!

This is an excellent series of paperback books, comprising
the very best classic material written about Holmes from
some of the most knowledgeable Sherlockians of all time.
Most of these books have never appeared in paperback
before, so Penzler has done Holmes fans a great service by
bringing these scarce and often pricey volumes from their
original hardcover editions out to the general reading public
in affordable and attractive quality paperback editions.

The books in this series are priced at $8.00 each (though a
few of the early volumes had $7.95 prices), and are regular
rack-size paperbacks — that is, standard paperback size.
They all have quality white paper pages and feature excellent
cover art by the great Frederic Dorr Steele — perhaps the
best illustrator of the Great Detective since the renown

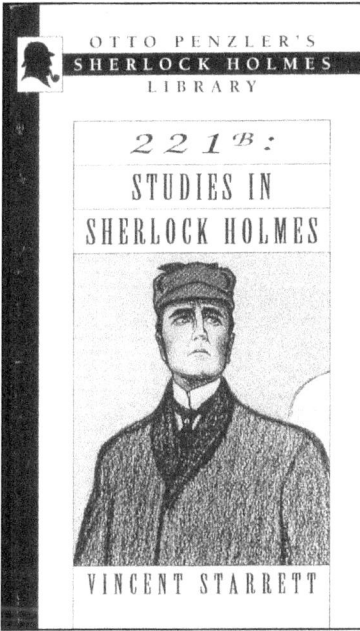

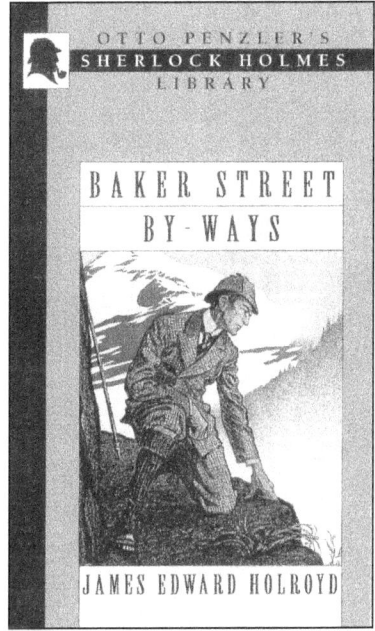

Sidney Paget. Though these books were priced a few dollars more than the average paperback on the racks at that time, the couple dollars difference is not important when you consider the quality packaging and the value you receive from the wonderful work between the covers of these books. The fact that now fans can purchase this long unavailable Holmes-related material at a reasonable price, rather than for (in some cases), hundreds of dollars in rare hardcover First Editions on the antiquarian or collector's market is an important consideration. Another added bonus is that many of these books were first published in England, some never having appeared in the United States in any form, and are thus First American Editions, and new to many American fans and collectors.

Otto Penzler is certainly to be congratulated for putting together this series and for having the sharp critical eye to pick out true classics that are the kind of high quality and timeless works that enhance everyone's enjoyment of The Canon. The Great Detective is very well served in this series

OTTO PENZLER'S
SHERLOCK HOLMES
LIBRARY

SHERLOCK HOLMES:
FACT *or* FICTION?

T. S. BLAKENEY

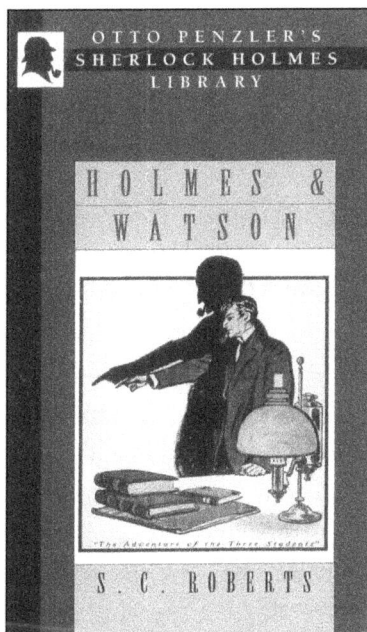

and these books have already become collector's items in and of themselves since they have first appeared.

There are nine books in the "Sherlock Holmes Library" series and they all have fine cover art by famed Sherlockian illustrator Frederic Dorr Steele. They are listed below with some information about each volume. Macmillan paperbacks were not widely distributed and I had to search around to find these books when they came out, today you might have to find a good out-of-print bookstore or Internet source to locate copies — but they are available. The books are certainly worth the search. These books are not numbered, but I have listed them here in the order of their date of publication.

#1: *The Private Life of Sherlock Holmes* by Vincent Starrett is the first book to appear in this series in late 1993. It's a Sherlockian classic and a fine and fascinating read. Starrett was a very knowledgeable devotee of the Great Detective and knew his stuff. The first and probably the last time this book was published in paperback was a Pinnacle

Books edition from about 1975. So, even though this Penzler paperback may not even be a first paperback appearance, it is a fine book that has been out of print for almost 20 years before this edition. It is about time that it was back in print.

#2: *Sherlock Holmes: Fact Or Fiction?* by T.S. Blakeney, comes in at 133 pages and came out in late 1993. It first appeared in hardcover in 1932, published originally by John Murray in London. This Penzler edition is the first paperback printing, and is probably the First American Edition. The book is a well-documented and researched study of Holmes and various areas of The Canon. It's well-written and I found it to be a fascinating read. Cover price was $7.95.

#3: *221B: Studies in Sherlock Holmes* edited by Vincent Starrett is the usual fine Starrett effort. This time he collected various works on the Great Detective that are sure to please. These include: "The Field Bazaar" by A. Conan Doyle; "Was Sherlock Holmes an American?" by Christopher Morley; "Nummi In Arca" by R.K. Leavitt; "On The Emotional Geology of Baker Street" by Elmer Davis; "Dr. Watson's Secret" by Jane Nightwork; "The Care and Feeding of Sherlock Holmes" by Earle F. Walbridge; "Three Identifications" by H.W. Bell; "The Other Boarder" by James Keddie; "Sherlock Holmes and Music" by Harvey Officer; "Sussex Interview" by P.M. Stone; "The Adventure of the Unique Hamlet" by Vincent Starrett; "Mr. Sherlock Holmes and Dr. Samuel Johnson" by Richard D. Altick; "Sherlock Holmes in Pictures" by Frederic Dorr Steele; "The Creator of Holmes in the Flesh" by Henry James Forman; "Appointment In Baker Street" by Edgar W. Smith; and "A Sherlock Holmes Cross-Word" by F.V. Morley. This book is 247 pages of sheer Sherlockian joy!

#4: **R. Holmes & Co.** by John Kendrick Bangs, from 1994, 231 pages, and is a first paperback printing of a novel which

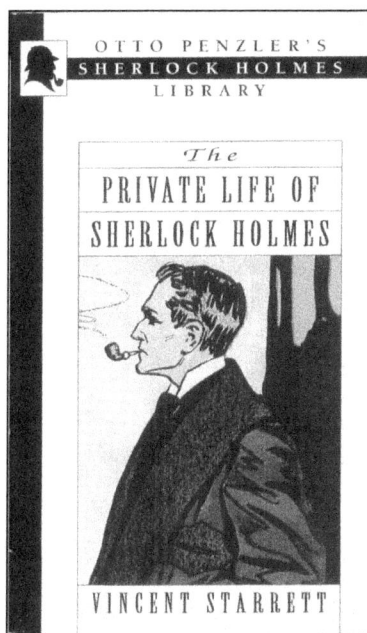

originally appeared in hardcover in 1906 from Harper & Brothers. Bangs was a fine writer, a popular author of his era, who wrote many excellent Sherlockian pastiches — among much other great works. This is one of his best, and until now, had been sorely neglected. This novel introduces Raffles Holmes, who is the son of Sherlock Holmes, and the grandson of the debonair thief, A.J. Raffles. It is an incredible saga in more ways than one! Nevertheless, Raffles Holmes tells this tale of his father Sherlock's pursuit of his thief uncle in this adventure set in 1883. It's a fun novel and contains six black and white illustrations reprinted from the original 1906 hardcover edition.

#5: *My Dear Holmes: Studies In Sherlock* by Gavin Brend, is a 183 page biography of Holmes that delves into many interesting questions. Originally published in 1951 by Allen & Unwin in the UK, this is the first paperback printing. The book also contains four illustrations and much material on all aspects of Holmes' life.

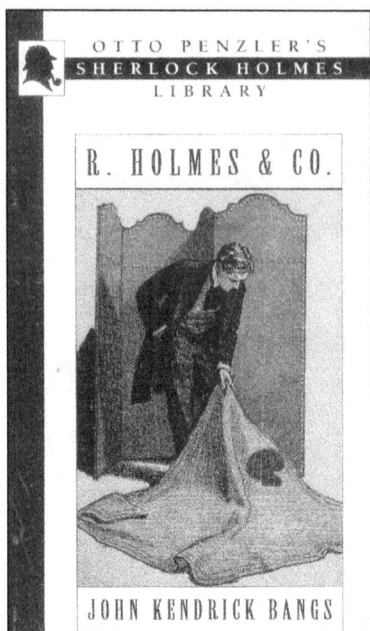

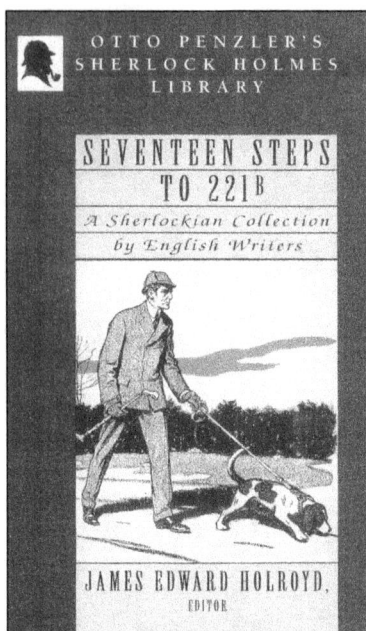

#6: *Seventeen Steps to 221B: A Sherlockian Collection By English Writers*, edited by James Edward Holroyd, contains a fine introduction by the editor, and is a 182 page first paperback printing. It was originally published in hardcover in 1967 by Allen & Unwin in the UK. This is a 17 story collection (one story for each step you must climb to Holmes' Baker Street lodgings). It includes Sherlockian pastiches by British writers, including Dorothy L Sayers; A.A. Milne; John Dickson Carr; and Adrian Conan Doyle (Sir Arthur's son). It contains seven illustrations and is a wonderful excursion into the early Holmes pastiche short story.

#7: *Baker Street Studies* edited by H.W. Bell. This is an excellent collection of essays on Holmes originally published in 1934. This paperback edition is from 1994, which I am sure will be much sought after and collectable.

#8: ***Baker Street By-Ways*** by James Edward Holroyd is from 1994 and reprint a 1959 UK hardcover from Allen & Unwin. The author talks about many things Sherlockian, including artists Sidney Page and Frederic Dorr Steele, and offers beloved overviews of the main characters in The Canon.

#9: ***Holmes & Watson*** by S.C. Roberts, originally published in hardcover by the Oxford University Press in 1953.This first paperback printing is from 1994 and is an entertaining collection of Sherlockian writings and includes two examples of Roberts' own charming pastiches: "Christmas Eve" and "The Strange Case of the Megatherium Thefts."

These nine books that make up "The Sherlock Holmes Library" are a joy for any mystery reader or fan who desires to find out more about our favorite detective hero. Otto Penzler has done a true service to all fans and collectors of Sherlock Holmes in this series of excellent and attractive books.

"The Lost World" & Professor Challenger in Paperback

O nly slightly less known than the great detective Sherlock Holmes, is Sir Arthur Conan Doyle's 'other' creation, the large, black-bearded volcanic, Professor George Edward Challenger. Challenger was a cantankerous curmudgeon and worldwide traveler and adventurer. A great scientist whose adventures were some of the best and most fantastic Doyle ever chronicled. Challenger was an uninhibited version of Doyle, according to mystery author and biographer John Dickson Carr.

The first and foremost Challenger tale was *The Lost World*, a thrilling tale of a journey back into time to a lost ancient world. Four men; Challenger, Summerlee, Lord John Roxton and the journalist, Malone, begin an expedition to a remote

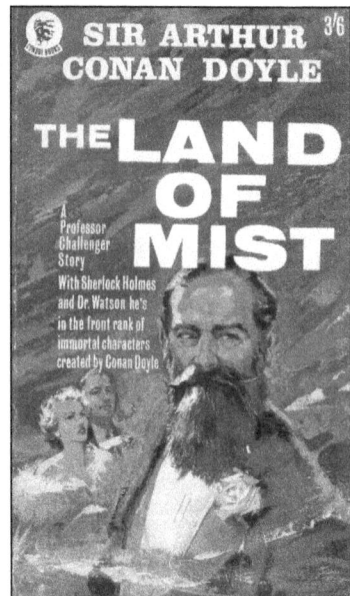

238 Sir Arthur Conan Doyle

THE LOST WORLD

35¢

A HARLEQUIN-PAN BOOK

NEWNES' COPYRIGHT NOVELS

The POISON BELT

A. CONAN DOYLE

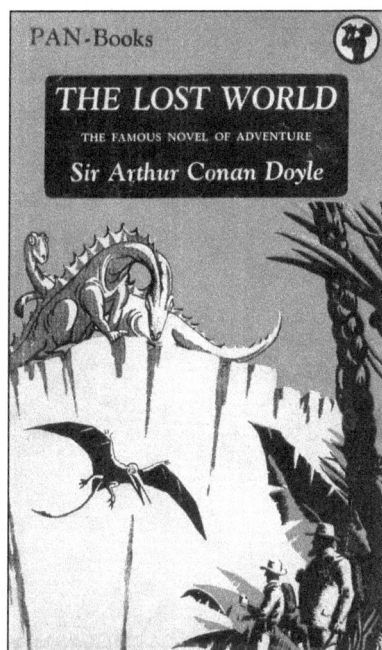

plateau in South America, cut off from the surrounding country by unscaleable perpendicular cliffs. They discover a world survived from prehistoric times, with giant flying pterodactyls and T-Rex and horrible ape-men. The idea for the tale was suggested to Doyle by the fossilized footprints of a prehistoric monster found near his home on the Sussex Downs (where Holmes would later retire and take up beekeeping). Doyle took the name of Professor Challenger from the wooden ship on which Sir Charles Wyville Thomson (the Zoology professor whose lectures he had attended when he was a medical student at Edinburgh University), who dredged the seas for new life. Challenger was one of Doyle's favorite characters. This classic novel was made into a masterful silent film, and later in the 1950s remade into a very popular film starring Michael Rennie and Claude Raines.

There are some wonderful paperback editions of this classic novel, most feature really excellent cover art showing fighting dinosaurs. The book seems to build on and update

tropes used in Jules Verne in his *Journey To The Center Of The Earth* and later used by Edgar Rice Burroughs in his novel *Pellucidar* and that series of later novels. Even *King Kong* has some features of this very influential novel in it.

The *Lost World* was originally written in 1911 and serialized in the *Strand* magazine in 1912. Probably the earliest paperback edition was a British Newnes edition, followed by a German (in English) Tauchnitz edition. I say probably, because I don't own copies of these books but since both publishers came out with many of Doyle's Holmes and non-Holmes works in paperback form I assume there could be editions of this novel from them. It seems unlikely they would have omitted this classic novel.

Mass-market paperback editions from America, England and Canada offer a fun and unique look at this novel and the characters in their cover art. Below is a listing of each edition with notes and information upon each.

PROFESSOR
CHALLENGER   IN

SECRETS OF THE
DREAMLANDS

Ralph E. Vaughan

Illustrated
by E.A. Geier

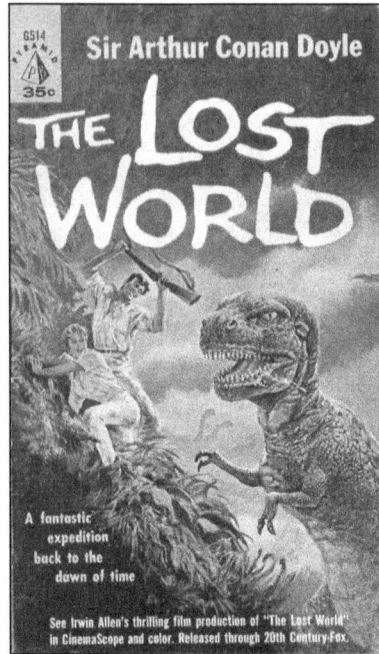

The Lost World In Paperback:

Pan Books, England, #100, 1st Pan printing 1949, 224 pp.

Pan Books, England, #100, 2nd Pan printing 1950, 224 pp, 2
   Shilling cover price. I assume the cover art on this edition is
   identical to the first printing.

John Murray, England, 1st printing, 1930, not much is known
   of these early Murray editions, they're extremely hard to
   find. I assume the 1930 and 1934 editions are paperbacks,
   but can't be sure. The 1960 edition is definitely a
   paperback.

John Murray, England, 2nd printing, 1934

John Murray, England, 3rd printing, 1960

John Murray, England, 4th printing, 1964

John Murray, England, 5th printing, 1969, great cover of
   Challenger and T-Rex which will become a kind of cover
   motif for this book used by various artists, 5 Shilling cover
   price, 215pp.

Harlequin Books, Canada, #238, July, 1953, 224pp, published

as a Pan-Harlequin Book, cover shows man in swamp and T-Rex behind him.

Perma Books, USA, Perma Star Book #279, Feb. 1954, 25 cents cover price, 200pp, outstanding and gory cover of rampaging ape-men, T-rex, dinosaurs and terror stricken men.

Pyramid Books, USA, #PR15, A Pyramid Royal Book, 1958, outstanding dinosaur fight cover by Ray Sternbergh, 35 cents cover price, 192pp.

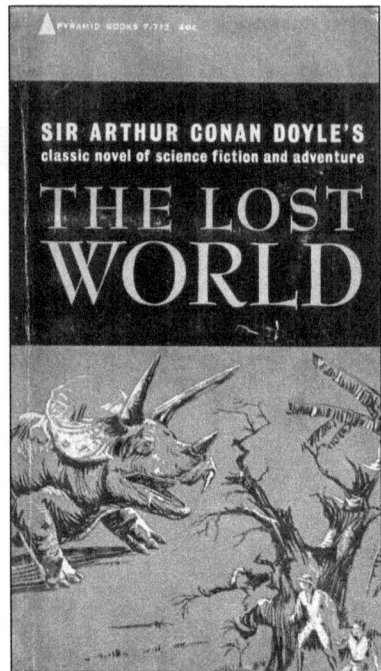

Pyramid Books, USA, #G514, 2nd printing June 1960, classic
   movie edition showing T-Rex attacking films stars
   Fernando Lamas and Jill St. John, also with Michael Rennie
   and Claude Rains, 35 cents cover price, 192pp, cover by
   Tom Beecham.
Berkley Books, USA, #?, 1st printing, Nov. 1965.
Berkley Books, USA, #?, 2nd printing, Dec. 1966.
Berkley Books, USA, #?, 3rd printing, Feb. 1969.
Berkley Books, USA, #X1826, 4th printing, Oct. 1969, 60
   cents cover price, 176pp, cover art uncredited, shows
   hunters shooting angry T-Rex.
Tor Books, USA, #812-53468-9, Nov. 1993, outstanding
   dinosaur cover by uncredited artist, $4.99 cover price,
   248pp.

   Challenger also appeared in the books *The Poison Belt* and
The Land of Mist. *The Poison Belt*, is a short novel originally
published in 1913. There were two short stories later, *"The*

Disintegration Machine" and *"When The World Screamed."*
All three were collected into *The Poison Belt* from Berkley
Books. These very underrated stories are actually science
fiction – Challenger transforms even further in these later
stories into the kind of science fictional super competent
scientist that Issac Asimov and Robert A. Heinlein would
write about so successfully decades later. I believe that
Doyle's Challenger presaged these future sf heroes. The
Berkley edition also has an interesting introduction by John
Dickson Carr. The Berkley Books paperback first printing
appeared in the USA, in April, 1966. It was reprinted in a
second printing as Berkley Book #X1827, Oct. 1969, with a
great cover showing Challenger and an angry red sky from
the title story of the book.

The Land Of Mist is the little known 'other' Challenger
novel, obscure and underrated in comparison with *The Lost
World*. I don't know if there was an American edition of this
but there certainly should have been. The copy I have was
published in England by Consul Books, #1212, from 1963, a 3
Shilling/6 Pence cover price and 223pp. It's a very
uncommon book.

Professor Challenger was a classic science fictional hero,
before Doc Savage, before Asimov's and Heinlein's
competent heroes, this large, black-bearded giant was a
scientist whose fantastic adventures thrilled millions.
Dwarfed by the popularity and stature of a more famous
detective creation, Challenger was a hit on his own. Had
Doyle written more Challenger stories, one wonders what
could have been.

The LOST WORLD
A. CONAN DOYLE

Illustrated with scenes
from the First National Picture

Lost works of "The Lost World"

Sir Arthur Conan Doyle's "other" famous heroic creation was the big, blustering, bearded, Professor George Edward Challenger. Challenger is anything but a "Sherlock Holmes" in style and temperament, but he is uniquely fascinating in his own way.

Challenger's greatest adventure was, of course, his descent into a strange and hidden South American jungle where he discovered a "Lost World". Here Doyle gave us a primitive world of prehistoric men and animals, and a rousing paleantology adventure novel.

The book was originally published in 1912, and was made into an incredibly popular 20th-Cewntury Fox film in about 1950 with Michael Rennie, Claude Raines, Fernando Lamas and Jill St. John.

However, before that 1950 film, about three or four decades before that, back in 1924, the book was also made into a fascinating *silent* film by First National Pictures. This early silent version starred a young Wallace Beery as Professor Challenger and Arthur Hoyt as Professor Summerlee. This film is one of those great old silent movie classics that has been lost to us today, almost as the Lost World lay

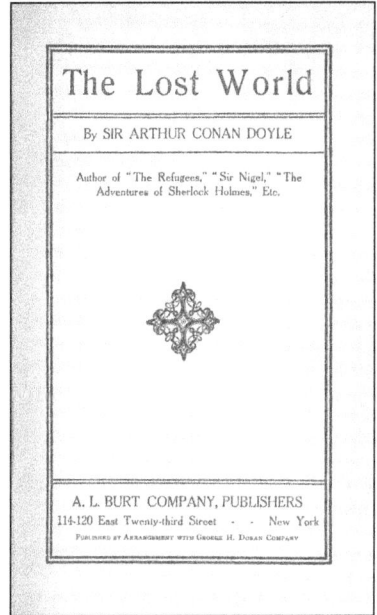

The Lost World

By SIR ARTHUR CONAN DOYLE

Author of "The Refugees," "Sir Nigel," "The Adventures of Sherlock Holmes," Etc.

A. L. BURT COMPANY, PUBLISHERS
114-120 East Twenty-third Street   ·   ·   New York
Published by Arrangement with George H. Doran Company

A midnight alarm awakens Paula White (Bessie Love), Sir John Roxton (Lewis Stone), Prof. Summerlee (Arthur Hoyt), and Prof. Challenger (Wallace Beery).
(The Lost World)   (A First National Picture)

undiscovered until Professor Challenger and his party came upon it. The film has excellent dinosaur fights that for the day were the height of cutting-edge early special effects of the era. This silent film is from 1924 and is hardly ever seen today and has become one of the lost classics of the early days of motion pictures. I've seen historical stills from the film, but never seen the actual entire film myself, but it looks impressive.

I'm also privileged to have a rare copy of the 1924 or thereabouts, A.L. Burt Photoplay edition of *The Lost World*. It's a beautiful hardcover book in gorgeous dust jacket. This hardcover is an early movie tie-in book and is illustrated with four full-page black & white plates that are stills from this silent film. It also features a stunning dust jacket that uses a nice black & white scene from the film that has been hand colorized.

Inside, opposite the title page, we are treated to a full-page photo from the film showing a battle between two mighty dinosaurs, an Allosaurus and a Trachadon. Meanwhile in the photo below and to the left, Profs Challenger (Beery) and Summerlee (Hoyt) look on with awe at the mighty struggle going on over their heads. This was pretty good special effects for any film in 1924 and this film photo is one of four that makes this Photoplay movie tie-in edition really special.

Another excellent photo is on page 215, where Paula White (Bessie Love), Sir John Roxton (Lewis Stone), and Profs Summerlee and Challenger are awakened at night by something in the trees above their camp. They look upward, aim rifles, and cringe in terror.

Prof. Challenger (Wallace Beery) and Prof. Summerlee (Arthur Hoyt) behold the death struggle between allosaursus and trachodon. (*The Lost World*)   (*A First National Picture*)

This A.L. Burt Photoplay edition of Doyle's *The Lost World* is scarce and in this superior condition with a complete and bright dust jacket, it may be rare. I wouldn't venture a guess as to dollar value, but it certainly must be about the $100+ range! It's a beautiful Doyle and dinosaur item, very collectable. It's the kind of special item that makes any collection shine and any collector's face smile. Like the silent film it chronicles, this early movie tie-in edition of *The Lost World*, is also kind of a lost work today. It has been lost in time and space, hardly ever seen, but not forgotten by collectors and fans of Doyle, and Professor Challenger and his amazing adventures.

The First Hard-Boiled Detective
The Strange Case of Birdy Edwards

The impact on the mystery field of Sir Arthur Conan Doyle has been enormous. Obviously, as the creator of the great Sherlock Holmes (and Doctor Watson) the world's first consulting detective, and the world's first "scientific" detective, Doyle has contributed to this field more importantly than most. However, there is another Doyle creation that may be just as important to the mystery field as is Sherlock Holmes, for which he has received no credit until now. That is the creation of the world's first hard-boiled detective!

Doyle's character is a true hard-boiled private eye and appears in the Sherlock Holmes novel, THE VALLEY OF FEAR. The detective is the wise-cracking, tough and resourceful American private eye, Birdy Edwards.

Edwards is a true hard-boiled P.I., a Pinkerton detective on an undercover investigation and is probably the first such detective to appear in print.

THE VALLEY OF FEAR was first published in 1915 in England, eight years before Carroll John Daly's

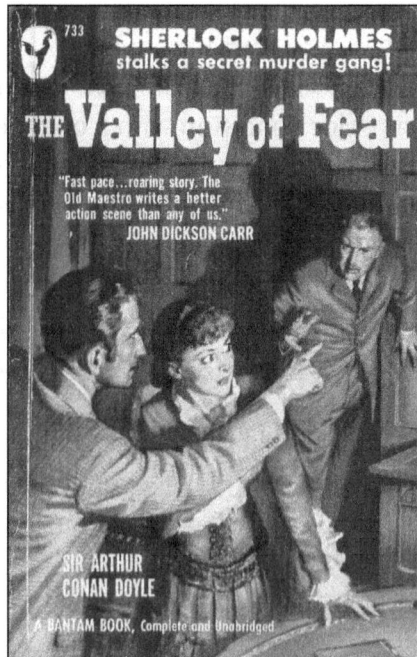

733 SHERLOCK HOLMES
stalks a secret murder gang!

THE Valley of Fear

"Fast pace...roaring story. The Old Maestro writes a better action scene than any of us."
JOHN DICKSON CARR

SIR ARTHUR CONAN DOYLE

A BANTAM BOOK, Complete and Unabridged

tough-guy Race Williams (1923), and six years earlier than Daly's Two-Gun Terry Mack (from 1921, and until now acknowledged to be the earliest incarnation of the hard-boiled detective in print). This is years before Dashiell Hammett and Raymond Chandler came on the scene with their own BLACK MASK stories. Though THE VALLEY OF FEAR was first published in 1915, the Birdy Edwards story, told in flashbacks in VALLEY, takes place in America in 1875, while the case at Brilstone Manor House for which Sherlock Holmes was called in to investigate actually took place some time in 1888. Coincidenty, that is the same year when Jack The Ripper was doing his 'work' in London.

THE VALLEY OF FEAR is the Sherlock Holmes novel that really wasn't — at least as far as some Holmes fans feel. This is to take nothing away from Holmes or Doyle, it's just that there's another story here that needs to be told. VALLEY begins naturally enough as the typical Holmes tale. We find Watson and his detective friend in their quaint lodgings in Baker Street, as a case is brought to their attention. It contains those unique characteristics that command the attention of the Great Detective. However, more than half of the book is told in a long flashback scene of many chapters about the goings on in a small Pennsylvania town under the thumb of the Scrowers, a hideous criminal secret society. Eight years later Carroll John Daly's Race Williams would fight a similar secret criminal society (that time it was the Ku Klux Klan sans

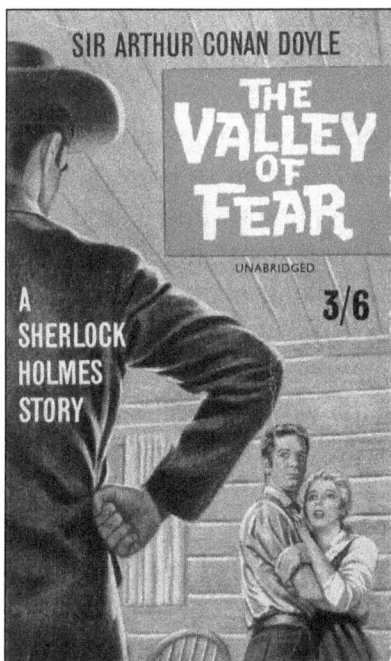

THE TRAPPING OF BIRDY EDWARDS

" 'Not a sound, for your lives!' McMurdo whispered."
Arthur I. Keller, *Associated Sunday Magazines*, 1914

much of their racism but as deadly organized criminals) in his first hard-boiled outing, "The Knights Of The Open Palm" (BLACK MASK 1923).

Birdy Edwards is an undercover Pinkerton operative. He'd been known as one of Pinkerton's best men and even some of the Scrowers have heard of his reputation and feared him. Edwards plays it tough and he plays it smart, in typical hard-boiled manner, sometimes wise-cracking, sometimes the wise-guy as he baits the local cops, but always the resourceful private dick who infiltrates the Scrowers undercover to bring them down in the only possible way. From the inside. Edwards is playing the most dangerous of games here, one where the smallest slip-up can mean instant death.

Birdy Edwards comes to the Vermissa Valley under the name of John McMurdo. He tells them he is out of the Chicago lodge of this nationwide fraternal society, which is basically a harmless and decent organization with lodges all over the country. However, in Vermissa Valley — in The Valley of Fear — the local lodges there use the supposedly harmless fraternal rituals and secret aspects of the lodge in a brilliant manner to create a criminal organization that thwarts police and enforces blind obedience and terror. Here the local lodges have been twisted into a vicious criminal enterprise of extortion and murder. The concept is really quite innovative for 1915 and shows Doyle's intuitive understanding of the ways of crime. He shows how crime and corruption can infect society, attacking it like a virus, until it has taken over the host like the disease it truly is. Doyle had Holmes have run-ins with similar types of secret societies in previous Holmes adventures, (such as the KKK in "The Five Orange Pips"), but Doyle outdid himself with this gritty tale of the vicious sinister Scrowers.

When Scanlan, one of his lodge brothers, asks why he left Chicago, McMurdo (Edwards) tells him:

> "I found plenty of work to do," said McMurdo.
> "Then why did you leave?"
> McMurdo nodded towards the policemen and smiled. "I guess those chaps would be glad to know," he said.
> Scanlan groaned sympathetically. "In trouble?" he asked in a whisper.
> "Deep."
> "A penitentiary job?"
> "And the rest."
> "Not a killing!"
> "It's early days to talk of such things," said McMurdo with the air of a man who had been surprised into saying more than he had intended. "I've my own good reasons for leaving Chicago, and let that be enough for you. Who are you that you should take it on yourself to ask such things?" His eyes gleamed with sudden and dangerous anger from behind his glasses.

Birdy Edwards, using the name John McMurdo infiltrates the Scrowers and finds out what they're all about. Before he reached Vermissa he was skeptical. The reports of what was going on in the Valley of Fear seemed too bizarre to be true. It seemed impossible that local lodges of such a harmless fraternal organization could have transformed into this dark secret criminal society built on extortion and murder. Yet Edwards' investigation uncovers a group of the most vicious killers this side of Capone's Chicago.

Furthermore, not only is Edwards a true hard-boiled P.I. but the very town of Vermissa is a typical hard-boiled place, a gritty, brawling, dirty mining town, set in a "Valley of Fear". Doyle describes it thusly as Edwards rides into the valley and sees it for the first time.

The country had been a place of terror; but the town was in its way even more depressing. Down at long valley there was at least a certain gloomy grandeur in the huge fires and the clouds of drifting smoke, while the strength and industry of man found fitting monuments in the hills which he had spilled by the side of his monstrous excavations. But the town showed a dead level of mean ugliness and squalor. The broad street was churned up by the traffic into a horrible rutted paste of muddy snow. The sidewalks were narrow and uneven. The numerous gas-lamps served only to show more clearly a long line of wooden houses, each with its veranda facing the street, unkept and dirty.

Here we have an early description by the British writer Conan Doyle of the typical "mean streets" of hard-boiled fiction which is as grim and depressing as anything Hammett or Chandler would write about many years later. And this was from 1915, and from the pen of an Scot, rather than an American!

" 'Stand back yourself!' he cried. 'I'll blow your face in
if you lay a hand on me.' "
Frank Wiles, *Strand Magazine*, 1915

I believe Birdy Edwards to be the first hard-boiled detective
to appear in fiction and that his true place of importance in
the mystery genre has been ignored until now only because
he was overshadowed by a much more famous "consulting
detective" also involved in the investigation of what had
occurred in the Valley of Fear many years previously.

Realization of this important contribution by Sir Arthur

" 'Hush, on your life!' cried the miner, standing still in his alarm,
and gazing in amazement at his companion."
Frank Wiles, *Strand Magazine*, 1915

Conan Doyle further augments his already mighty status in
the mystery field, making him, in fact, the true spiritual
father of a long run of hard-boiled detectives and private
eyes that would continue years later with Two-Gun Terry
Mack, Race Williams, Sam Spade, Philip Marlowe, Mike
Hammer — all the way to current popular detectives such as
Spencer and even V.I Washawski.

Furthermore, though some American fans and scholars
might object, a strong case can be made that since Birdy
Edwards is the world's first hard-boiled detective in print —
the origination of the entire hard-boiled detective sub-genre
of the mystery field must now move away from America —
and to England! Thus we have the first hard-boiled detective
being created by a *British* author, from Scotland, and first

published in *England*!

I think genre fans and scholars may have quite a bit to say about this for years to come.

The story in THE VALLEY OF FEAR concerns the Scrowers long arm of revenge against Birdy Edwards. McMurdo (Edwards) has trapped the leaders of the society at his rooms in a house in Vermissa by telling them he has had word of an undercover Pinkerton named Birdy Edwards who is on their trail. McMurdo tells Boss McGinty and his henchmen how he can trick this Edwards to come to his rooms so they can all fall upon him and find out just what he knows about the society.

With McGinty and his band of killers in the next room, McMurdo sets the "trap" for Birdy Edwards. The prearranged signal of three knocks to the downstairs door finally comes as McMurdo answers the door. Voices are heard in the hall. Finally McMurdo enters the adjoining room where McGinty and his men are laying in ambush, and in a dramatic scene confronts McGinty:

"Well!" Cried Boss McGinty at last. "Is he here? Is Birdy Edwards here?"
"Yes," McMurdo answered slowly. "Birdy Edwards is here. I am Birdy Edwards!"

With this revelation there is chaos, but Edwards (as McMurdo) has been working all along with the company police and the Scrowers are quickly rounded up and arrested. As a result of Edwards later court testimony the leaders of the Scrowers are sent to the gallows or imprisoned and this criminal society is broken. Nevertheless, from that moment on the long hand of what remains of the Scrowers sets after Edwards on a hell-bent mission of revenge.

Remnants of the group track Edwards down to Chicago where he is forced to flee. They track him to the California gold fields, and he makes his escape again. Finally, after some thirteen long years they track him down to England, where Birdy Edwards is now retired and has been living for some time under yet another assumed name. This time he is John Douglas, the squire of Brilstone Manor House. This is the case that Sherlock Holmes is called on to help solve after Mr. Douglas' apparent mysterious murder.

At the conclusion of the case "John Douglas" is found alive by Holmes, and he and his wife escape once again having to leave England.

Later, in an epilogue to the story (and the case), Holmes and Watson receive a visitor with a telegram informing them that Mr. Douglas (the name Edwards was using while in England) was lost at sea in a storm on a ship making its way to South Africa. Though it is not stated he was murdered and thrown overboard, Holmes says of the incident to Watson:

"There is a master hand here. It is no case of sawed-off shotguns and clumsy six-shooters. I can tell an old master by the sweep of his brush. I can tell a Moriarty when I see one. This crime is from London, not from America."

"But for what motive?"

"Because it is done by a man who cannot afford to fail, one whose whole unique position depends upon the fact that all he does must succeed. A great brain and a huge organization have been turned to the extinction of one man. It is crushing the nut with the trip hammer — an absurd extravagance of energy — but the nut is very effectively crushed all the same."

Birdy Edwards is that tough nut to crack. A hard-boiled P.I., and the best of the Pinkertons. (Coincidentally, Dashiell Hammett was himself a Pinkerton at this very time, working as a detective for the agency from about 1914 to June 1918 out in Montana). But Birdy Edwards was the best of the

'Pinks'. It would take Moriarty and his far-flung "huge organization" (the quote is from Holmes), to finally bring him down, and that was only after what remained of the Scrowers had been chasing him for thirteen years over two continents.

Birdy Edwards and THE VALLEY OF FEAR deserve a second look by all Sherlockians and all fans of hard-boiled fiction. The fact that many Sherlockians regard TVOF to be the weakest of the Holmes stories may be because, in fact, it is not *really* a Holmes story at all, but a Birdy Edwards story! In that context I believe it merits a deeper look and Birdy Edwards should be elevated to his rightful place in the genre as the first hard-boiled detective. And Sir Arthur Conan Doyle should be acknowledged as the true founder of the hard-boiled detective story.

One wonders what might have been had Doyle written another Birdy Edwards story? Perhaps of his earlier days as a 'Pink' in Chicago?

Epilogue:

Just as there was an Epilogue to THE VALLEY OF FEAR where Holmes brought us up to date on Birdy Edwards' fate after he left England, I wanted to include my own short epilogue to the Strange Case of Birdy Edwards.

So what of Birdy Edwards after THE VALLEY OF FEAR? Was he, in fact, murdered and thrown overboard by Moriarty's henchmen as Holmes mentions at the end of the story? Or did Edwards once again fake his own death to throw his enemies off his trail? I am sure that only Sherlock Holmes knows the true answer to that question, but if the latter is true, Sherlock Holmes would not be the one to give the game away, now would he? And Watson would not write the truth of any escape by Edwards in his story of the case!

The Molly Maguires:
The REAL Birdy Edwards
in the REAL Valley of Fear!

This article is a sequel of sorts to my previous
examination of Sir Arthur Conan Doyle's Sherlock
Holmes novel, *The Valley of Fear ("The First Hardboiled
Detective: The Strange Case of Birdy Edwards"* originally
published in *The Armchair Detective*, Spring 1994 issue and
reprinted in the *Shoso-in Bulletin* in Japan).

It all begins apparently harmlessly enough. There was at
one time in the coal mining areas of Pennsylvania in the late
1800s a fraternal organization, that was in fact a criminal
gang. They were a vicious, brutal group of murderers known
as the Molly Maguires.

There was a film based on the organization and their
crimes and terrorism activities that came out in 1969. The
film starred Sean Connery, Richard Harris and Samantha
Eggar. There was a movie tie-in paperback original by James
O'Neill, based on the film screenplay by Walter Bernstein
(Gold Medal Book #R2168, 1969). The book and film are
fairly accurate accounts of what actually took place in the
mining towns of Pennsylvania in the later 1800s.

From the back cover of the Gold Medal paperback:
"Exploited by the owners, brutalized by the police, the
impoverished miners of the rich Pennsylvania coal fields
were driven to savage dreams of reprisal. Their only hope lay
in the Molly Maguires, a secret band of Irish terrorists.

"James McParlan smiled, drank, and fought his way into
their confidence. To the tough young detective, it was just
another job. He did not think of himself as an informer, a
Judas. Nor did he think of the desperate men who would die

A Fawcett Gold Medal Book

R 2168
60¢

THE MOLLY MAGUIRES

A novel by
JAMES O'NEILL
Based on the screenplay by
WALTER BERNSTEIN

Now a Triumphant Paramount Picture starring
RICHARD HARRIS SEAN CONNERY SAMANTHA EGGAR
A MARTIN RITT PRODUCTION

because of him – until he met Mary. Innocent, trusting, beautiful Mary. Would he have to destroy her too?"

A bit overly dramatized, but you get the point.

The true story of the Molly Maguires, was also the true story that Doyle used as a basis for his Holmes novel, *The Valley of Fear.* Doyle based his novel on this actual historical criminal incident in America that he heard about which led him to write *The Valley of Fear* as history.

Many readers and Holmes fans alike find *The Valley of Fear* to be the Holmes novel that really *isn't.* What it is actually, is the story of Birdy Edwards and his investigation of the criminal 'Scrowers' gang. In fact, many readers find the American section of *The Valley of Fear*, telling of Birdy Edwards's adventures in the Vermissa Valley in the mining area of Pennsylvania uninteresting and incredible. Which is strange because that is the most interesting, even fascinating section of the book since it not only chronicles a true story, but an incredible and little-known incident in American history. It's a fascinating story because it is not a story — but true. Every event in Doyle's novel was taken directly from actual events.

The miners of the Shenandoah Valley (Doyle calls it the "Vermissa Valley") of Pennsylvania were among the most oppressed workers in the world at that time. Workers lived in company towns that were little better than prison camps, 12 hour days were the norm, no overtime pay, no health plan, no vacation, no retirement unless you died — then you could retire. The companies didn't care how they treated the workers because there were always more workers where those came from. Most workers were immigrants who were only too happy to have that job. There were no strikes. It was not a happy place.

The Irish, who were more organized than most workers with their fraternal societies, decided to do something about it. The Irish immigrants, and we're talking Catholic's, were kept out of the mainstream, so they had their own organizations, much like the later Italian immigrants would have their own ("Black Hand" and the "Mafia") decades later to fight for their rights – presumably – and to exploit them, eventually.

Regardless, there were already thriving fraternal Irish organizations in the valley like the Ancient Order of Hibernians (who Doyle would translate into the "Eminent Order of Freemen" known as the "Scrowers"). The workers could always find a pub or house to get together to talk about problems on the job.

This is not the first time that Doyle used this device in a Holmes story. He used another secret and criminal organization, the Ku Klux Klan in his story "The Five Orange Pips." The Klan, an evil and racist criminal organization, grew out of the Masons from the post Civil War American South. So again we see where a secret organization sprang up from the depths of an open one.

Irish legend tells of the heroine Molly Maguire, a stirring resistance leader who fought for Irish freedom against the hated Brits. So, the oppressed miners of the Shenandoah became Sons of Molly Maguire, later shortened to Molly Maguires (Doyle calls them, the "Scrowers").

The Molly Maguires began by beating up the oppressors. Usually foremen. They had so-called "action teams" who did the dirty work and a group of members who would provide alibis for anything the action teams did. These well-alibied teams — the Mafia with their *Omerta* had nothing on these *boyos* — then began killing foremen and blowing up mines. Things were soon getting out of hand.

The man who became the leader of the Molly Maguires was a bold fenian tough named "Black Jack" Keyhoe (Doyle calls him "McGinity"), who is called the Bodymaster of his group. Such terms as Bodymaster of the Scrowers were taken directly from the actual occurrences as Keyhoe was Bodymaster of the Molly Maguires.

The railroads, which owned half the country back then and

incidentally also owned the mines began to strike back. One day, into this valley of fear, the Shenandoah valley where the mines operated, came James McKenna (Doyle calls him "Jack McMurdo") a counterfeiter on the run from Buffalo (not Chicago as Doyle tells it) after having killed a man there. McKenna begins making acquaintances among the Irish miners, and having a reputation as a ruthless man, became known to the Molly Maguires as just the sort of fellow who might like to join up. Just their kind of guy. History shows that not only was there a real James McKenna but he actually became the personal secretary of Bodymaster Keyhoe. He was up and rising and on the inside track for success but he was also aware of certain other things. Such as the fact the railroad and the mine bosses had had enough of the killings and explosions. This oppression and terrorism was a terrible thing from the point of view of the mine bosses, and besides, they were supposed to be the ones on the *giving end* of it, not the *receiving end*. Something had to be done.

What was done was the railroad and mine bosses hired the "We Never Sleep" Pinkerton Detective Agency, who after the Civil War ended, augmented their case load by doing labor-busting and acting as goons for company bosses. Pinkerton HQ sent in their top "Pink" to handle the case, a guy by the name of James McPharlan (who Doyle renamed "Birdy Edwards").

So you see Doyle, aside from changing a few names of the key players, based his Holmes novel *The Valley of Fear* upon a true historical incident. In many ways, Doyle kept to the historical script, but in some ways – and I've often found this in the more fascinating stories in history – the truth is even more fascinating and outrageous than the fiction based upon it! It is amazing but true. I once wrote a story about the hunt for a man-eating tiger that had caused such devastation among the people of India (verified kills were over a thousand!) the editor felt he had to cut the number down to a few hundred kills because the readers just wouldn't believe it. But it was true, and you can look it up in *The Guinness Book of World Records* under man-eating tiger attacks.

The same kind of thing seems to have happened with Doyle's retelling of the Molly Maguires. The true story is even more fascinating than his fiction based upon it.

What were some of the differences between the Doyle story and the actual historical event? Well, first of all, while Birdy Edwards in the Doyle story infiltrated the Scrowers for about six months – the real investigator, McPharlan stayed under cover for an incredible *four and a half years!* Which, of course, in real life, gave him the opportunity to travel up and down the valley to all the other lodges, knowing Bodymaster Keyhoe's business inside and out. It was also said that McPharlan was an incredible womanizer and that he had a girl in every town. One point Doyle did not use in his fictional account.

When it all came apart, unlike his fictional counterpart, the historical baddy, Bodymaster Keyhoe went to the gallows for murder and a lot more. Afterwards James McPharlan lived out his days, without having to go into hiding as Doyle had Edwards do (of course, that was the basis for the Holmes part of the detective novel that took place years afterwards in England). Edwards was hiding out in England as Mr. Douglas at the opening of Doyle's story.

Other Molly Maguires were hanged or imprisoned and the gang was broken up. And while McPharlan lived afterwards without any problem, another informant *was* killed. Interestingly enough, he was thrown over the side of a ship off the coast of South Africa! Just as, supposedly, Doyle has Edwards (as Mr. Douglas) thrown over the side of the ship he was on with his wife which just happened to be off South Africa.

However, there's even more. The hit man, who was a Scrower or working for them was in real life was a master killer who was known by the name *"The Avenger!"* Shades or

Moriarity for real? He was caught though. As Moriarity was not.

I think that aside form all the other data presented you need go no further than the very interesting end of *The Valley of Fear* to see that Doyle did in fact base his Holmes novel on this obscure bit of American history. In fact, Doyle seems to have gone quite a bit farther than merely basing his story on this incident. It begins to look suspiciously like he almost copied the tale outright, turning it into a Holmes story. And it worked.

At the end of *Valley*, Edwards (now calling himself Douglas) is supposedly murdered by Moriarity (or one of his henchmen), when in reality the murder was committed by this "Avenger" hit man. Then coincidence of both the Molly Maguire informant and Douglas (Edwards) thrown over the side of a ship off the *South African* coast – well, to say that Doyle was *"influenced"* by this story of the Molly Maguires seems a bit of a stretch. It seems more likely Doyle copied the history outright. Oh, for sure he changed a few names, but he seems to have copied almost item for item the true story of the Molly Maguires and I think that's an interesting story in and of itself.

However, the most interesting story is the actual court testimony of Mckenna and the other informants and the reports of McFarlan that came out during the prosecution of Keyhoe and the other leaders of this American criminal and early terrorist organization and was used to hang them. The list of beatings, killings, sabotage was long and dark and the inside workings of the Molly Maguire organization was fascinating and terrifying. A dark side of America that is as obscure today as in Doyle's day. A blot on American history that was left to Doyle, a Brit, to bring to light in his great Birdy Edwards and Sherlock Holmes crime novel, *The Valley of Fear*.

An Appreciation of John Bennett Shaw

We are lucky when we encounter a person of exceptional qualities, and one such gentleman was John Bennett Shaw. He was a man who supported everything and everyone Sherlockian. A friend, mentor, fan and master collector, who was always most generous in sharing his vast knowledge and advice to anyone interested in the Great Detective. That is why the loss of such a giant is so heartfelt and missed.

I had not heard of the death of John Bennett Shaw on October 2, 1994 until I read of it in THE SHOSO-IN BULLETIN (Volume 5, Aug. 1995 issue, a very well-regarded Japanese Holmes magazine). It was very sad news. John Bennett Shaw will always be remembered by me as "The Man," and I say that with all sincerity and respect for The

John Bennett Shaw

Canon and as a Sherlockian, because Shaw was most definitely the world's greatest living Sherlockian of his era.

John Bennett Shaw was a scholar and collector of world renown, and he allowed his collection to be used to further the study and appreciation of Doyle and Holmes. Shaw's collection was so vast and broad that even formed the basis of Ronald B. De Waal's excellent world bibliography of the Great Detective (De Waal wrote a touching letter about Shaw in the above issue of *The Shoso-In Bulletin*). De Waal writes eloquently of the friendship and help he received from Shaw while working on his massive book, his visits to the man, and his research and study of Shaw's incredible and extensive Sherlockian collection. That truly must have been an adventure all by itself.

I knew John Bennett Shaw briefly, and only from his letters to me through the mail, and because of the introduction he was kind enough to write for my own extensive bibliography on The Canon, SHERLOCK HOLMES: THE GREAT DETECTIVE IN PAPERBACK & PASTICHE (Gryphon

Books, 1990; which was reprinted in an updated/expanded full-color edition in 2000). I will always regret not meeting John face to face and of missing the opportunity to view his wonderful collection.

I found John Bennett Shaw to be a true gentleman, and a very supportive friend and a kind of mentor who encouraged me and my work on that book. It meant a lot to me for someone of John's great knowledge and evident stature in the field to take an interest in my minor puny undertakings. But that was John Bennett Shaw, a tireless advocate for anything Sherlockian, always supportive, always the fan, a collector, a scholar, a sharer of information, and a good friend. He was also a very nice fellow with a good sense of humor. His letters to me, though written by an older gentleman late in his life always glowed with that same wonder and energy, that same kind of buoyant enthusiasm he must have felt when as a small boy so long ago he had read his very first Sherlock Holmes story. That same wonder and joy was always there.

With the passing of John Bennett Shaw that joy and wonder has not left this world, even as our world is so much richer for his having been amongst us. John Bennett Shaw has left his precious gift of joy and wonder to each one of us who knew him and remember him still.

And always.

Sherlockian Odds and Ends: Part 1

A few years ago, actually more than a decade ago – time really *does* fly – I wrote and published a small Sherlockian booklet called **Relics of Sherlock Holmes**. The book was a chatty attempt to list some of the recent 70s and 80s Holmes material I ran across then. Such as articles, ads, news, cartoons and other of the *less* major works on the Great Detective.

Relics of Sherlock Holmes was published in 1988 and reprinted in

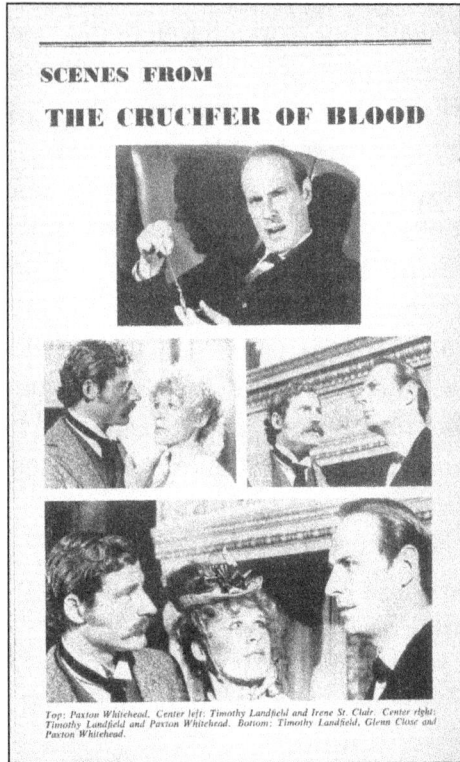

SCENES FROM
THE CRUCIFER OF BLOOD

Top: Paxton Whitehead. Center left: Timothy Landfield and Irene St. Clair. Center right: Timothy Landfield and Paxton Whitehead. Bottom: Timothy Landfield, Glenn Close and Paxton Whitehead.

1992. It was a fun book to do, it sold well, but has gone out of print. In the meantime, I've come across a few Holmes odds and ends that I thought I would list here in this article. It begins with two of the better and more obscure Holmes films and one short story fiction pastiche.

Hands of a Murderer, was a good Holmes film. I have a full page ad that ran in *TV Guide* for the original CBS TV movie which aired Wed. May 16, 1990 and starred Edward Woodward as Holmes and John Hillerman as Watson. Holmes fights Moriarity for top military secrets in this

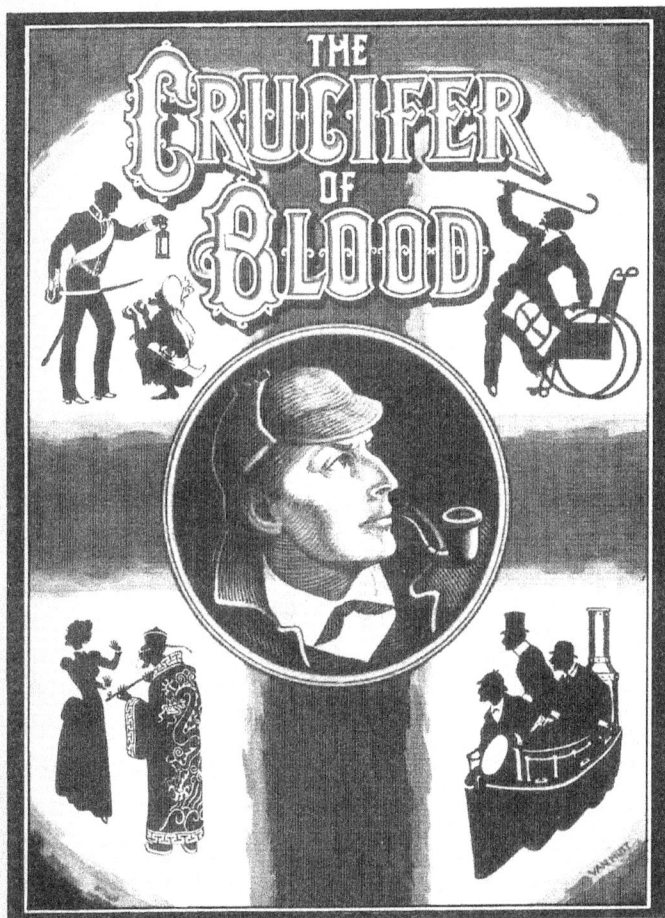

"SHERLOCK HOLMES FANS, REJOICE!"
—THE HOUSTON POST

MICHAEL P. HODEL AND SEAN M. WRIGHT

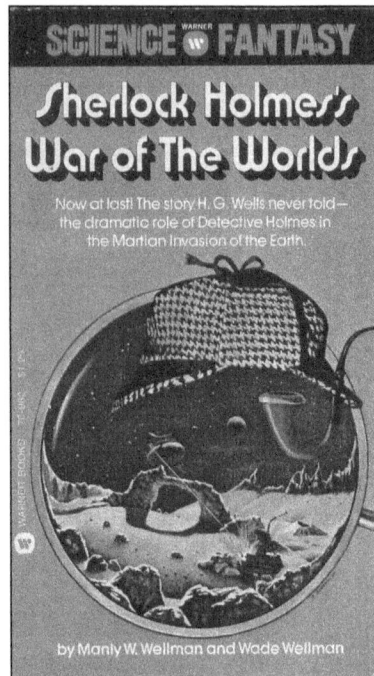

SCIENCE ⓦ FANTASY

Sherlock Holmes
War of The Worlds

Now at last! The story H. G. Wells never told—
the dramatic role of Detective Holmes in
the Martian invasion of the Earth.

by Manly W. Wellman and Wade Wellman

original story. It was pretty good fun. Mycroft appears. Not a bad pastiche film and one that I don't believe has ever been re-run on TV. I wonder why?

The Crucifer of Blood, was originally a play, but it later appeared as this TV movie. I have another full page ad that ran in *TV Guide* for this original TNT movie which aired Nov. 4, 1991. It starred Charleston Heston as Holmes with Richard Johnson as Watson. It wasn't a bad portrayal either. Heston, who has played everyone from Moses to Ben Hur and a bunch of other historical figures did a credible job on this story which originally had been a Broadway play. There was also a slim Doubleday hardcover. The play and later book were both written by Paul Giovanni. The ad shows Heston as Holmes with pipe in the traditional pose. This is another Holmes film, and a lesser known Heston film. I don't believe I've seen it re-run on TV. I wonder why, again?

"The Worcester Enigma" is a new Sherlock Holmes short story pastiche that originally appeared in *Mystery*

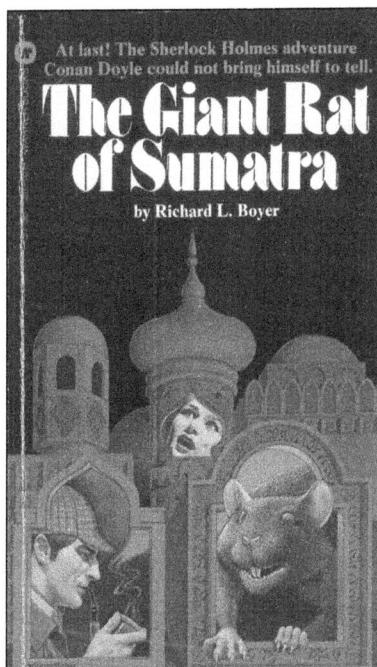

Magazine, March 1981 issue, which was their excellent Sherlock Holmes issue. This five page original short story pastiche is great fun and not all that well known. I don't believe it has ever been reprinted either.

There are a lot of pastiche films and books that continue the adventures of Holmes and Watson. I've written about a lot of them in various articles over the years and in my book **Sherlock Holmes: The Great Detective in Paperback & Pastiche**, which appeared in a new, expanded and updated edition in late 2000. It was loaded with new material and had a full colro cover and inside pages. In doing all the research for this book I came across a lot of excellent pastiches, and I've listed a few favorite paperback editions.

Two of my favorite older and more obscure films are: **They Might Be Giants** with the great George C. Scott as a slighty off-center judge who thinks he may be Holmes, and Joanne Woodward as his shrink by the name of Watson, who begins to believe he might *just* be Holmes after all. It's a wonderful romp, filled with a lot of 60s social consciousness, but a sweet film with a lot of heart. And George C. Scott is great. It's a lot of fun.

Sherlock Holmes in A Study In Terror, the Ellery Queen film (and movie tie-in paperback original) is loads of fun. A nice, older, classic Holmes and Watson on the case of Jack the Ripper. I really liked this film for its simplicity and it tried to be a good standard Holmes film in the style of the Basil Rathbone flicks of two decades earlier. It's a good transitional film to the newer and more distaff Holmes films of the 70s and 80s, such as **The Seven Per-Cent Solution** and even, **Murder By Decree**. All three of which are films I like very much. Of course, Rathbone is the best Holmes ever, with the exception of Jeremy Brett, who was simply terrific! William Gillette? Well, he was way before my time, but more importantly there are no films with him as Holmes available for comparison so it's hard to say just how good he was. I know he was accounted as simply Great in his day, but...

When it comes to Holmes pastiche novels, some of my favorites are **Sherlock Holmes In the War of the Worlds** by Manly Wade Wellman and his son Wade, a fine and exciting retelling of H.G. Welle's epic Martian invasion with Holmes at the center of it. Professor Challenger is thrown in for good measure. Great fun! I also really loved Richard L. Boyer's classic **The Giant Rat of Sumatra**. The 'story for which the world was not yet prepared' is everything Doyle's (and Holmes') implication promised in the capable hands of Boyer. He is a fine writer and even better, a very innovative one. This is a wonderful Holmes novel and great fun. These two books are well known by Holmes fans and have become cult classics.

I also got a big kick out of **Enter The Lion**, with Mycroft and Sherlock battling a Confederate coup in the US. Also, the two pastiches by Loren Estelman featuring Dracula and Dr. Jekyll were fun. Fred Saberhagen's paperback original pastiche Dracula novel, **An Old Friend of the Family** was great fun. An unacknowledged classic! There are a lot of others I have enjoyed over the years.

And now, for the one Holmes short story pastiche I have never read but wish I could read more than anything else!

It began with hints and rumor. I confirmed it some years ago when I was corresponding with George MacDonald Fraser the world-famous author of the wonderful Flashman novels. I was corresponding with him about an issue I was working on at the time of my collector's magazine ***Paperback Parade*** (#22), which was devoted to him and his work. I asked him about the rumor of a short story I heard he wrote where Flashman meets Sherlock Holmes. Supposedly the two work together on a case. Perhaps, and this is just surmise, Flashy takes the place of Watson in that case? If so, Holmes is in real trouble — if you know Flashman!

The story was indeed real, and it was published about 1970 in a British newspaper. There was no fanfare at the time, copies are impossible to find. After that lone appearance, Fraser has never allowed the story to be reprinted. I do not know why. I have never read it. I think it must be one of the most unique, rare, interesting and desireable of all Holmes *and* Flashman items. Of which I collect both. The story is almost a legend today. I would love to have a copy just to read. Fraser, a fine writer and a perfectionist, may not want it reprinted. Perhaps, at the time there was some problem with the Doyle estate? I don't know for sure. Or perhaps he may believe it is not up to his usual high standards. It's an early work after all. However, I'm sure that latter can not be true. Enjoying Fraser's work and his sharp wit as I do, I'm sure the story would be a fine tale. I know it must be hilarious fun.

So that's the one Holmes story this fan wishes he could get his hands on to read. Anyone out there got a copy? A xerox? Anything? A Flashman and Holmes fix is a tough combination to kick – but then, *who'd want to kick it!*

Sherlockian Odds & Ends Part II:
Flashman and the Tiger

It is so ironic and coincidental that one is almost ready to admit that some mysterious force might be at work – for as I was writing the very words that you have just read, a new Flashman book was published in the UK (Harper Collins) in October 1999. It was titled *Flashman and the Tiger*, and the book contains one novel and two short stories. The final story in the book, which is also the title story of the book, turns out to be the incredible Sherlockian Flashman romp I have written about previously in these pages. It must have been *kismet!* Glory! Yin and Yang coming together into perfect harmony!

Fraser, in a letter to me dated 1989 mentioned the story and that he was holding it aside for eventual publication in a Flashman collection. That volume of the Flashman Papers, as they are called, was finally published and a rousing adventure it is.

"Flashman and the Tiger," the Sherlockian story, concerns Flashy's plot to murder Tiger Jack Moran — or as he is more well known in the Sherlockian canon, Colonel Sedastian Moran. The evil and dangerous man who is second in command under the dread Professor Moriarity, involved in a vast world-wide criminal enterprise, called the second most dangerous man in London by Holmes himself, and the man who tried to – and damned well nearly did – assassinate Sherlock Holmes.

It's 1894, Flashman is over 70 years old now but he's lost none of the personal traits that made him the man he was in his younger days. A coward, a lecher, and a rogue. He has decided now that he has no choice but to commit murder, the murder of Tiger Jack Moran, to save the honor of his 19 year old

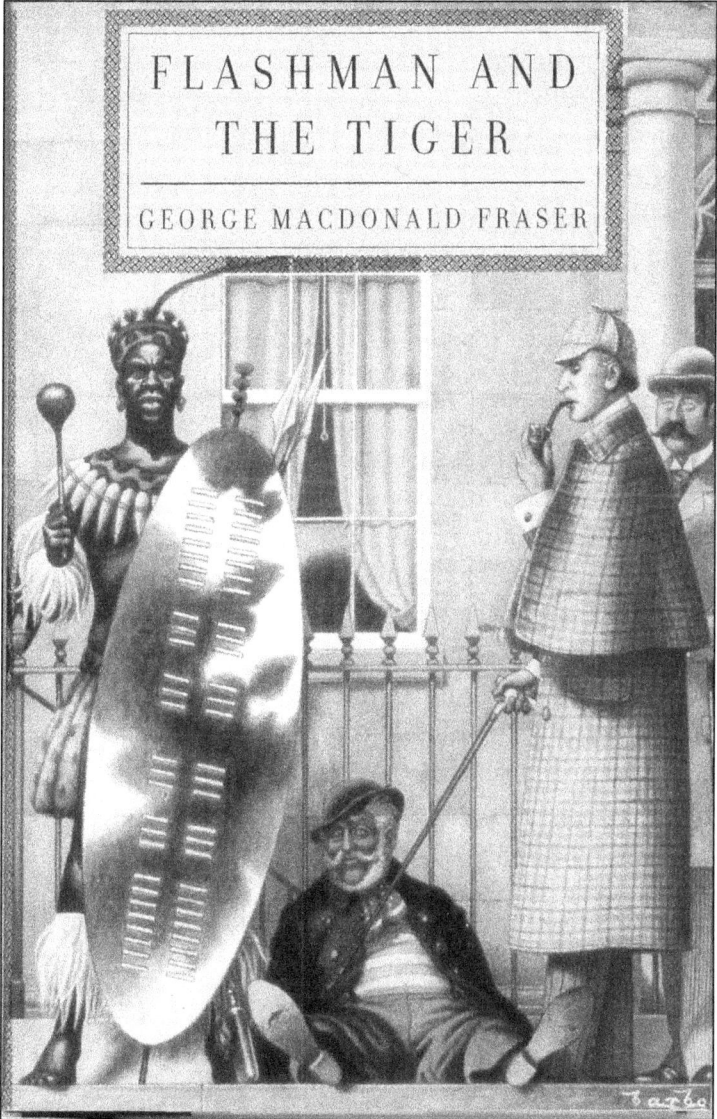

FLASHMAN AND
THE TIGER

GEORGE MACDONALD FRASER

granddaughter, Selina. Irony of ironies — and Flashy is the first to admit this - is how a man with no honor should be willing to commit murder for the honor of another.

The story actually began in 1879 where Flashy recounts his 'retreat' at the battles of Isanawana and Rorke's Drift in South Africa against the Zulus. Chased by bloodthirsty Zulu warriors, he meets up with Tiger Jack Moran. Flashy first impression of the man is a very careful, "Well, well, thinks I, here's one to keep an eye on."

After the battle there is a hiatus of 25 years until their next meeting in 1894. At that time Flashy is at the opera with his beloved granddaughter Selina, the apple of the old codger's eye. There Oscar Wilde introduces Flashman and Selina to Moran. The two men lock eyes. Flashy has a bad feeling about the man but dismisses it.

A few weeks later all of London society is shocked by the murder of the Honorable Roanld Adair. Now we find ourselves thrust knee-deep into a Flashman (and Fraser) version of the Sherlock Holmes case chronicled by Doctor Watson *as "The Adventure of the Empty House"* (see *The Return of Sherlock Holmes* by A.C. Doyle).

The story is the usual fun Fraser romp with Flashman and Holmes meeting finally at the end. Though not in any way you'd expect. It turns out that Flashy, the perpetual coward, was hiding out and spying on Moran disguised as a passed out drunken bum. After the capture of Moran, Holmes and Watson come upon the bum and Holmes stops to give Watson a long and brilliant recitation about this passed out 'sailor' – which of course turns out to be totally *wrong!*

Fraser has fun with the Holmes myth here. Flashman's impressions of Holmes: "an amazing lunatic," "a know-all ignoramus," and finally, "a conceited ass." Not all that complementary to the Great Detective, but after all this is a Flashman story, and it is Flashy's version of the events, and if you are familiar with Flashy you know he holds nothing back and is a scoudrels scoundrel! Thing is this is a fine fun romp and this older Flashman is still in fine form and just as much a coward, lecher and charming rogue as his younger self ever was.

By the way, Flashy saves his beloved granddaughter's virtue from the evil Moran. Only to have her throw it away on the lecherous 'Beastly Bertie' (Albert, Prince of Wales) of whom Selina is now his mistress. And as if to add insult to injury, Selina and the prince are doing the dirty deed in a secret apartment Flashy let's the prince use for his female assignations. Or as Flashy says, "…oh, she was Flashy's little grandchild all right, every inch of her."

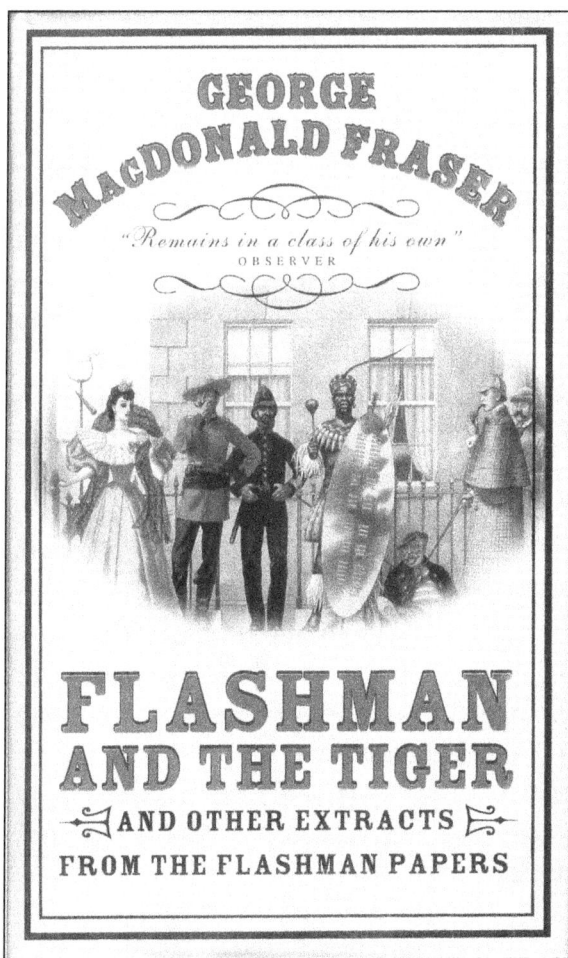

On The Broadway Stage: "Sherlock's Last Case"

I am a Holmes buff who generally likes his Sherlock to be no-nonsense and pretty close to the Doyle original. Excepting that ideal, however, I will accept and often enjoy the brilliant interpretations of the Great Detective as portrayed by Basil Rathbone; especially in his earlier Holmes films. I even have to admit, that unlike many dyed-in-the-wool Sherlockians, I've also enjoyed Nicholas Meyer's interpretations of Holmes in the novels *The Seven Per-Cent Solution*, and *The West End Horror*. And the film featuring Nicol Williamson as Holmes was not at all that bad either. After all, it was still Holmes, and it was all in good fun, even though it was a far cry from the original Doyle version. However, he spirit, if not the intention was still there, and it was still the same Sherlock we all enjoy and love.

And the love and enjoyment of that character is the main point with any newer Holmes work. And that brings us to the play, *Sherlock's Last Case*, a classic Broadway play which I saw performed at the Nederlander Theatre in New York City way back in 1987. It seemed to be a different situation altogether. For while the play had many positive aspects to recommend it, there were dome serious problems with it as well, in my opinion. And to me, these were problems that spoiled the play for me, and perhaps for many other true believers of the 'Sacred Canon'.

I generally love plays, and a Sherlock Holmes play is always something special that I want to experience, though some of the scenes in *Sherlock's Last Case* had me shaking my head in shock and disbelief. I watched as our beloved

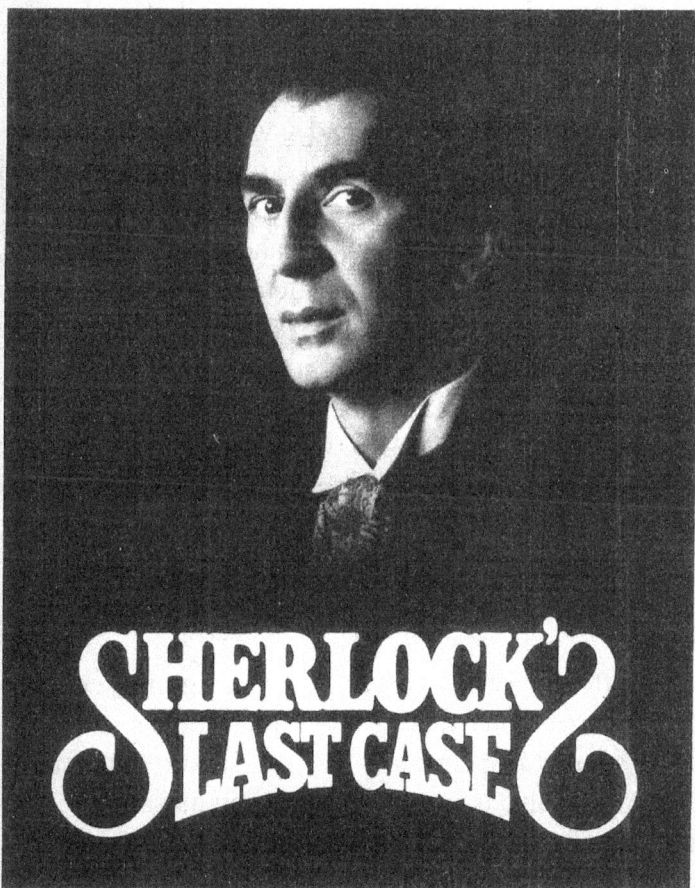

PLAYBILL®

NEDERLANDER THEATRE

SHERLOCK'S LAST CASE

Holmes was played yo characteruresque excess to become a
man who bore little or no relation to the Great Detective we
all know and love. In other scenes I sat askance, watching a
character whose base cruelty, coldness, and lack of any
moral fiber could do nothing but elicit hatred from the
audience or any true Holmes fan. Was *this* Sherlock Holmes?
No! It certainly was not!

I am the type of Holmes fan who is irresistibly drawn to any
new book, movie, or play featuring the Great Detective. In
that fanaticism I know I am not alone. This can lead to many
wonderful experiences as you can imagine, but many
disappointments as well.

Sherlock's Last Case was a lavish Broadway production,
featuring magnificent scenery and staging, effective use of
lighting and staging, and very competent performances from
all the cast. The special effects were very well done,
effectively bringing the atmosphere and mood of 1890's
London, as well as the feeling and detail richly alive in the
Baker Street lodgings. All this, and done on a relatively small
stage was a wonderful accomplishment.

Just as effective were the sets. One featured a revolving
stage used to change scenes between acts, and the manner
in which the stage was made into an underground chamber
was intriguing, with a ceiling that doubled for the surface of
the ground above. It created an interesting bi-level stage
effect that brought quite a few gasps from the delighted
audience.

This is, after all, Broadway, and staging, lighting, costumes,
and acting are all on a quality and professional level.
Sherlock's Last Case certainly had all of that to its benefit —
and more — it also had stage veteran and master actor,
Frank Langella, in the lead role as the Great Detective
himself.

Langella's Dracula of years previous (another play that was
a Broadway hit and then made into a popular film) was a
wonder, and a magnificent acting job that was amicably

Top: Frank Langella and Melinda Mullins. Middle left: Frank Langella and Donal Donnelly. Middle right: Donal Donnelly and Frank Langella. Bottom: Pat McNamara, Donal Donnelly and Frank Langella.

suited to Langella and given full justice by him as well. He presented a blood-curdling sexual fascination as Dracula.

Langella's Holmes was a well-acted effort, and did shine in spots, but the main problem as I see it with Sherlock's Last Case (and this latest version of Holmes), was the script itself. There were too many implausible premises that simply would never occur (and should never occur), in a play that even faintly follows The Canon. Chief among these is the unrelenting jealously an hatred of Holmes, by, of all people, good, loyal Watson! Totally out of character!

And as if this was not bad enough, Watson actually plans and carries out the *murder* of Holmes — and he damn near brings it off! This was not only out of character, but actually insulted many Holmes fans, or at least the serious ones.

But it gets only worse, before it gets batter. Langella (in a chief fault of the play that must be blamed on the script), portrayed an extremely cold, pompous, stingy and very cruel Holmes — a man constantly putting down Watson and Mrs. Hudson in the most base and derogatory terms. His treatment of Mrs. Hudson I found particularly disturbing and distasteful, and as unfair to that character as it was to the original version of the Great Detective himself.

While Donal Donnelly played an amiable Watson in the beginning — more in the vein of an older, but thinner Nigel Bruce — he soon metamorphosed into a veritable monster, an insanely jealous creature consumed by hatred for his great mentor to the point that he even tries to kill him. Now I ask you, is this creature the true Doctor Watson? Not in the least!

Meanwhile the audience was tortured by a Holmes who showed a cruelty of character that was not at all pleasant to see — a cruelness that Doyle would ever have permitted. The sad result of all this is an actual hatred of this great literary hero by the audience — in an elaborate staged even that is the epitome of an anti-Holmes play. I can only wonder what that part of the audience thought of this version of the Great Detective who had never encountered the original — or even an accurate pastiche version of the great man.

It was a shame that with so much talent and experience behind this production, the play turned out to be such a travesty. If you really know and love the Doyle characters; the valiant Holmes, the loyal Doctor Watson; the motherly love and attention that Mrs. Hudson represents; and insist on some measure of authenticity in these pastiche works, then *Sherlock's Last Case* will prove to be a major disappointment.

When I first viewed this play many years ago, during the middle of its Broadway run on a Thursday night, the house was only half full, and I recall feeling vaguely uneasy about this. After all, at the time this was a new Sherlock Holmes play, and this was Broadway in New York City! However, as the play progressed and my sensibilities were shocked again and again by outrageous out-of-character dialogue, attitudes, and plat direction — I began to see that perhaps word-of-mouth had got out about the play.

Sherlock's Last Case was certainly *not* for strict Sherlockains. In fact, ironically enough, I believe that the *less* you know about Doyle's illustrious creation, the *more* you might enjoy this play. Unfortuantely, the reverse is also quite true as well!

As I sat there in the audience, quiet, thoughtful, at the play's end, I realized that perhaps the play might have been more effective, and even fun, if it had been done a a non-Sherlockian murder mystery reminiscent of Deathtrap. Otherwise, an extensive rewrite might bring Holmes, Watson, and the plot more into authentic character — though I somehow doubt it with this particularly terrible script.

AS it turned out, Sherlock's Last Case did not break any new ground, though it may be trying to do just that with the shocking aspects of the story. Unlike the book and film versions of Meyer's The Seven Per-Cent Solution, which at least offered something new and interesting in the interplay between Holmes and Sigmund Freud, this Broadway offering does not shed any light on one of the greatest fictional characters of al time. Sorry to say, Sherlock's Last Case was a disappointing production that had a hard-edged cruelness to it. The entire event was unpleasant.

A Brief Look At:
Sherlock And The Count

The following play review was written very many years ago, and originally published in my booklet Relics of Sherlock Holmes, *about a play that was way off-Broadway and seemed to have been much, and unjustly, ignored at the time. A famed Holmes scholar once mentioned to me more years ago than I would care to admit, that he believed that my short article was the only review or mention of this obscure play in print. I thought that it should be reprinted here to give that play some recognition.*

It was a long time ago, the tale of which I am going to tell you now. It was in New York City, in an off-off Broadway theatre on a cold windy night of March 23, 1983. It was a perfect wintry night for the monumental battle that was to occur, and a great time was going to be had by all.

What I am talking about is the play, *Sherlock Holmes Embattles Count Dracula*, which was written by Fred Fondren and had a week run at the Prometheus Theatre at 239 East 5th Street in New York City in March 1983. The tickets were a modest six dollars.

This was an original Holmes play written by Fondern which captured quite well the personality of Holmes and Watson, along with the atmosphere and mood generated by the original Doyle stories. Fondren wrote the play, and he also played the part of Sherlock Holmes extremely well, with respect for the character which easily came through to the tiny audience. Fondern also directed. The job of acting on one's own play and directing it at the same time can be very difficult, to say the least — that Fondern pulled off all these jobs so well speaks highly of his talent and the high quality of this play.

The story concerned, Lady Sofie, the daughter of the King of Bohemia (who was a prior client of Holmes some years before). It has become Lady Sofie's sad duty to wed a suitable royal consort thereby producing an heir for the kingdom. Needless to say, her consort is of the royalty — a count, in fact — a fella by the name of Count Dracula! Well, Lady Sofie has some second thoughts about this mysterious and enigmatic count, and seeks out Holmes and Watson to investigate this Dracula before he becomes a part of the ruling family of her beloved country.

The acting by all members of the cast was quite professional, while props and lighting, which transformed the tiny storefront theatre (this was after all off-off Broadway) into a accurate and eerie stage and create some realistically believable sets. Though a tiny production, *Sherlock Holmes Embattles Count Dracula* was none the less a well-done labor of love and a serious attempt to portray Holmes accurately and humanely, by a group of talented actors and actresses who obviously care very much about doing the best job on a small shoe-string budget.

Well, it's all over and gone now, a play I saw almost 40 years ago, but one that has never been forgotten. As I have said elsewhere, I like my Holmes to be Doyle-traditional, with no fantasy or fantastic elements — but sometimes something comes along that is so good, so special, that it must be recognized for the quality and joy it gives the viewer — and that in it's own way is loyal to Holmes and Doyle. We can hardly ask for more. This play was just as well done as any big-budget Broadway Holmes play — but of course on a far smaller scale — and is a lot more obscure. My aim here is that this tiny article will not allow such a fine piece of obscure Sherlockania to slip away from our collective consciousness without some of the recognition and praise that it and all connected with it, truly deserve.

Epilog:

From where I sit writing this in early 2022, I do recall that when I saw the play it was in a small storefront theatre, with only 20-30 other people and we were each given a slim program – but being a person who saves everything Sherlockian – I have not been able to find it for this book. That happens sometimes, with collectors. However, through the kind assistance of Sherlock Holmes fans and collectors Peter Blau and Evy Herzog, I was sent a cover image of the very scarce program for this obscure play and it is reproduced here. I have since discovered that the Prometheus Theatre was a former motorcycle shop in the East Village, in New York City. The stage was tiny, just 9 by 12 feet. The theatre was founded by Fondern, and a closer friend, and they did many plays there over the years.

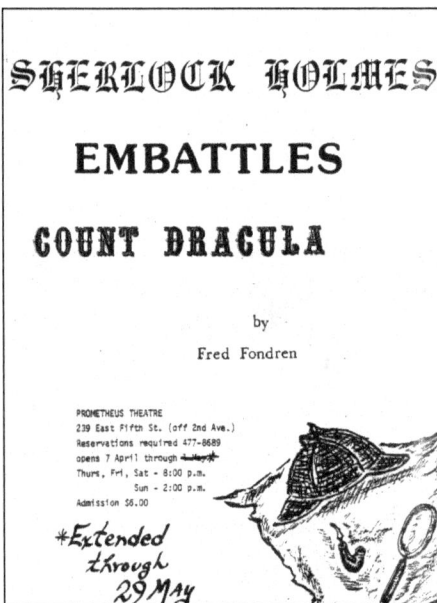

SHERLOCK HOLMES

EMBATTLES

COUNT DRACULA

by
Fred Fondren

PROMETHEUS THEATRE
239 East Fifth St. (off 2nd Ave.)
Reservations required 477-8689
opens 7 April through ~~July 3~~
Thurs, Fri, Sat - 8:00 p.m.
          Sun - 2:00 p.m.
Admission $6.00

*Extended
through
29 May

Fred Fondern was born in Alabama in 1948 and appeared in the 1993 film, *Joey Breaker*. He played the role of a man dying from AIDS. He himself died from AIDS in 1992, and the movie was dedicated to him. Fred Fondern was just 44 years old. So sad to die so young. I did not know him, I never met him, but I do want this article to be a tribute to him, and this wonderful and original Sherlock Holmes play. I hope that it achieves that aim, and that perhaps, some day, his play may be revived.

Notable Holmesian Pastiches & Other Oddities

Most mystery fans know that the first Sherlock Holmes story, "A Study in Scarlet" was published in the 1887 issue of *Beeton's Christmas Annual*, a magazine – but few fans know that the first Sherlock Holmes *book* was in fact, a paperback. In 1888 the British firm of Ward Lock & Co. reprinted *A Study in Scarlet* in a very rare paperback edition. It is considered more rare even than the *Beeton's* magazine version, of which a copy sold a while back for $50,000! That paperback was the first Sherlock Holmes book. It began a long line of Sherlockian publishing in softcover that continues today over 120 years later. A facsimile was published in 1993 in a 500-copy edition and that has also become collectable. Here then, is a sampling of Sherlockian highlights, oddities and rarities.

Canonical: Books By Doyle:

One of the earliest series of canonical Holmes books (collecting the original stories written by Doyle) were those published by Tauchnitz Books. Beginning around 1893 with *The Adventures of Sherlock Holmes*, this German firm specialized in reprinting books by American and British authors for expats and tourists in Continental Europe. All the books were printed in English but were not for sale in America or the British Empire due to copyright restrictions. They had plain text covers and are uncommon. All Tauchnitz Books by Doyle are scarce and very collectible.

"Pirates" or pirated editions also abounded since America was not a signature of the Berne Copyright Convention —

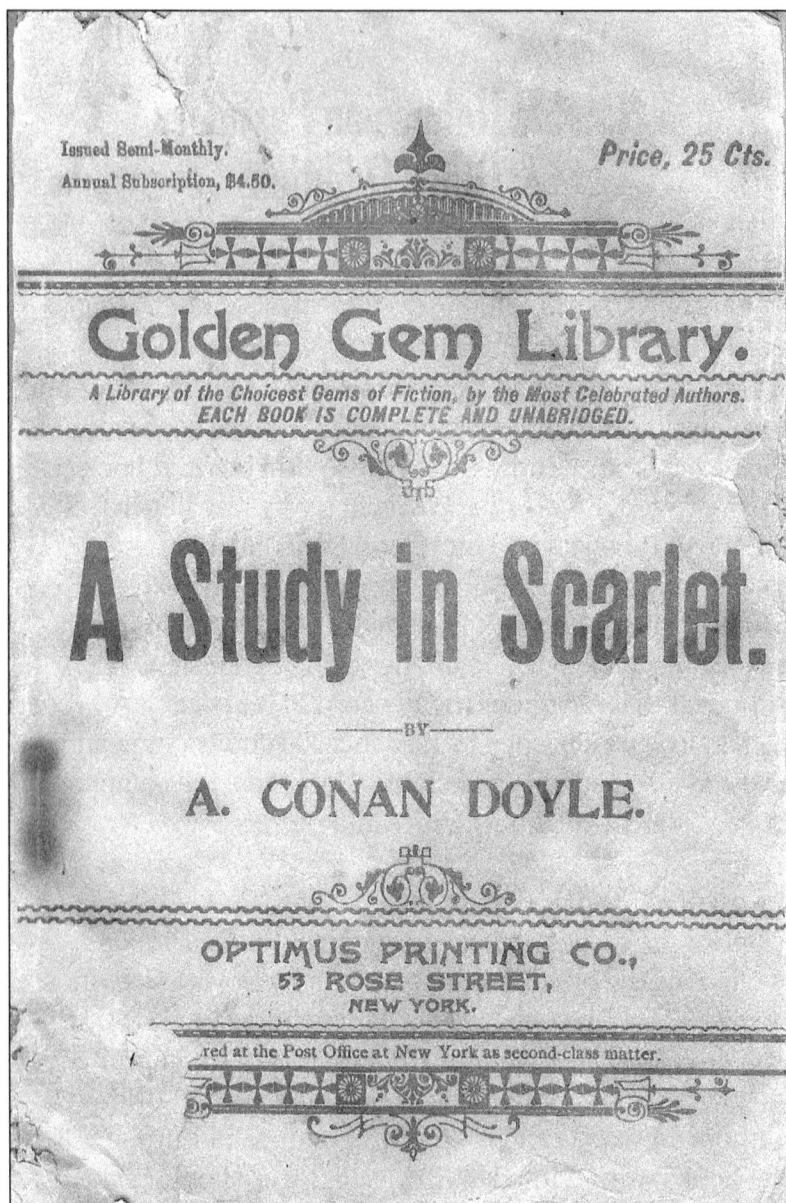

Issued Semi-Monthly.   Price, 25 Cts.
Annual Subscription, $4.50.

Golden Gem Library.

A Library of the Choicest Gems of Fiction, by the Most Celebrated Authors.
EACH BOOK IS COMPLETE AND UNABRIDGED.

A Study in Scarlet.

————BY————

A. CONAN DOYLE.

OPTIMUS PRINTING CO.,
53 ROSE STREET,
NEW YORK.

...red at the Post Office at New York as second-class matter.

publishers did not pay foreign authors to reprint their work.
One interesting American pirate edition was A *Study in
Scarlet* from the Golden Gem Library, #17 from April 25,
1892, which had a plain text cover in gold lettering. A later
version of the same book from the Arthur Westbrook

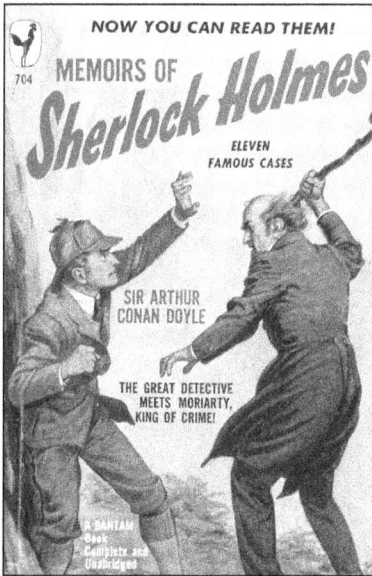

Company of Cleveland, Ohio, was published circa 1900-1910 and had an early illustrated cover.

Pocket Books was the first American mass-market paperback outfit to reprint a collection of Holmes stories in *The Sherlock Holmes Pocket Book* (Pocket #95, 1941), a first edition collection. It was reprinted many times with the same cover art but the 11th printing in 1944 had a new cover. That variant edition is very scarce.

Bantam Books reprinted three Holmes books in mass-market paperback beginning in 1949 with *The Hound of The Baskervilles* (Bantam #366). This edition showed sexy bondage cover art by William Shoyer more in keeping with the pulp-style popular at the time than having anything to do with our Mr. Holmes. More on target was *Memoirs of Sherlock Holmes* (Bantam #704, 1949) with the cover art showing a traditional battle between Holmes and Moriarty; and *The Valley of Fear* (Bantam #733, 1950) showing Holmes and Watson.

British paperbacks also offer some wonderful cover images, editions from John Murray and Pan Books are popular with collectors. *The Valley of Fear* (Pan Book #177, 1951) has cover art by Philip Mendoza that shows Holmes and Watson reading a letter – or secret message! *The Return of Sherlock Holmes* (John Murray, 2nd printing, 1960) shows Colonel Sebastian Moran using his notorious air-gun to assassinate Holmes in a scene from "The Adventure of the Empty House".

In 1956, the Western Publishing Company produced

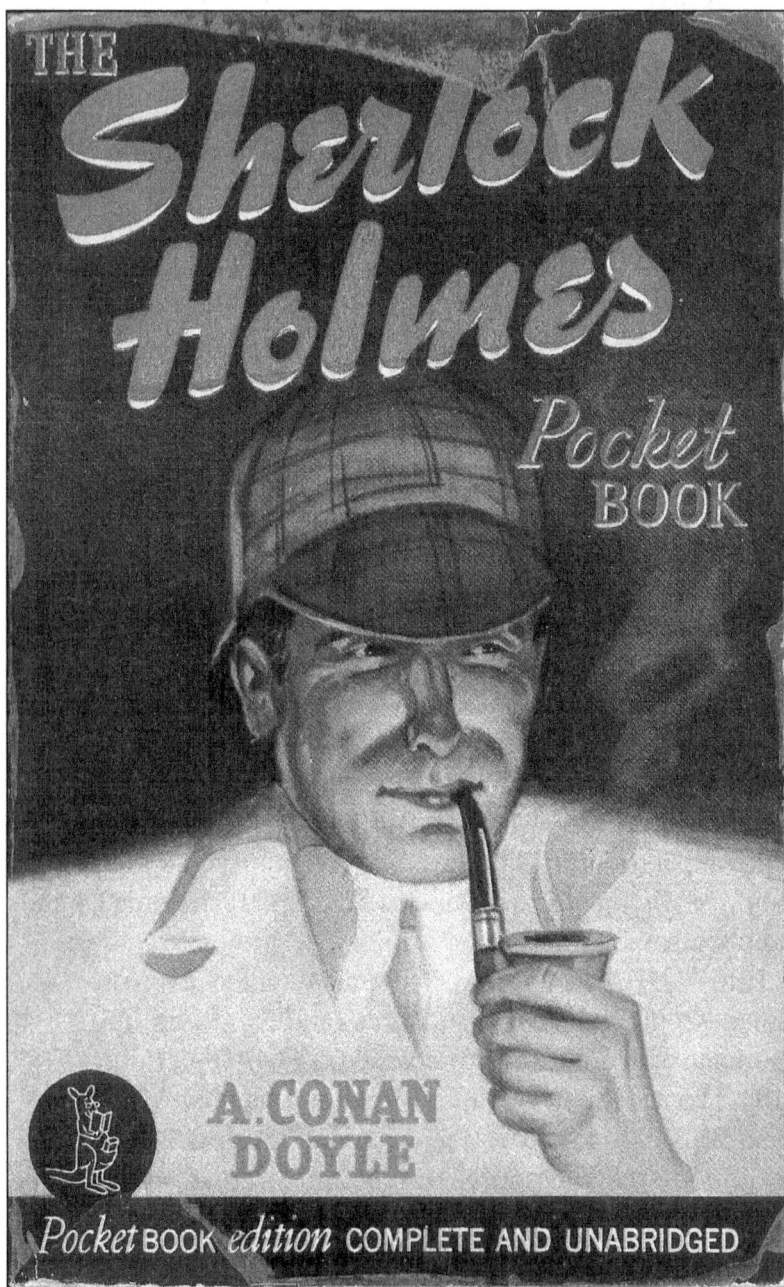

THE *Sherlock Holmes* *Pocket* BOOK

A. CONAN DOYLE

Pocket BOOK *edition* COMPLETE AND UNABRIDGED

Sherlock Holmes, a nicely done collection of stories that was a give-away from Nestles Chocolate. It also appeared in 1968 in a couple of different formats, but always with the same cover art. It has since become scarce.

Pastiches: Not By Doyle:

The pastiche is a time honored form of literature – done in the style of another artist. From the earliest days of Sherlock Holmes the popularity of the Great Detective led to a plethora of pastiche tales. In the early days, at the turn of the 20th Century, copyright restriction caused Sherlockain pastiches (and parodies) to feature detective heroes with the most unlikely names – Herlock Sholmes, Padlock Jones, Hemlock Coombs, and more. Diehard Sherlockians wrote their own tales that continued the adventures, or addressed the dozens of intriguing cases mentioned by Watson in The Canon that had been left untold, or to retell existing stories in new and different ways.

Once the copyright on the Holmes stories expired in the 1970s a floodgate was opened up and the first book to take advantage of this new reality was Nicholas Meyer's bestseller, *The Seven Per-Cent Solution*. The book was a Dutton hardcover from 1974, but what a lot of fans and collectors don't know is that there was a rare Advanced Reading Copy published by Dutton months earlier in illustrated warps (trade paperback size), with the same David K. Stone cover art which would later appear on the first edition hardcover. Meyer's book really jump-started the Sherlockian pastiche writing craze which has become a sub-genre, and some may say a mini industry, all its own today. Meyer went on to write three more Holmes pastiche novels but none attained the success of his first Holmes book. However, many more writers would step up to fill the breach, some who are well-known names in the mystery, science fiction, fantasy and even horror fields.

Two of what I consider to be the best and most entertaining

Holmes pastiches are mystery writer Richard L. Boyer's *The Giant Rat of Sumatra* (Warner Books, 1976) a paperback original and his first book – it tells a tale "for which the world is not yet prepared." Fantasy author Manly Wade Wellman (with son, Wade) offers a classic in *Sherlock Holmes's War of The World*s (Warner Books, 1975). This later book is made up of four connected short stories, two originally appeared in *The Magazine of Fantasy & Science Fiction*, and two were original tales, making this a first book edition and a paperback original. It tells the story of the Martian invasion of Earth after the H.G. Wells story. It is well done and great fun.

One of the best and most highly regarded of Sherlockian pastiches are the Solar Pons stories written by August Derleth. Derleth began the series in fond imitation of Doyle's detective with the short story "The Adventure of the Black Narcissus" in 1928 when he was just 19 years old. Over the years he expanded the series into 7 wonderful books (six collections and one novel, *Mr. Fairlie's Final Journey*) chronicling the adventures of Pons and his sidekick, Dr. Lyndon Parker. The books were originally published in hardcover by Mycroft & Moran, an imprint of Derleth's own Arkham House. In the 1970s, Pinnacle Books reprinted the series in an attractive set of paperbacks. In the 1980s, Pinnacle commissioned UK author Basil Copper to continue the series with four additional original story collections that are getting difficult to obtain.

Mystery author Stuart Palmer is also known for two well-regarded and enjoyable pastiche stories in *The Adventure of the Marked Man and One Other* (Aspen Press, 1973). This slim and uncommon volume was limited to only 500 copies as are many small press, fan press, or scion society items. In fact, some of these more off-trail items are limited to only 221 copies, some even under 100 copies!

Science fiction anthologist and mystery maven Kingsley Amis wrote one pastiche and it is also well-regarded; *The*

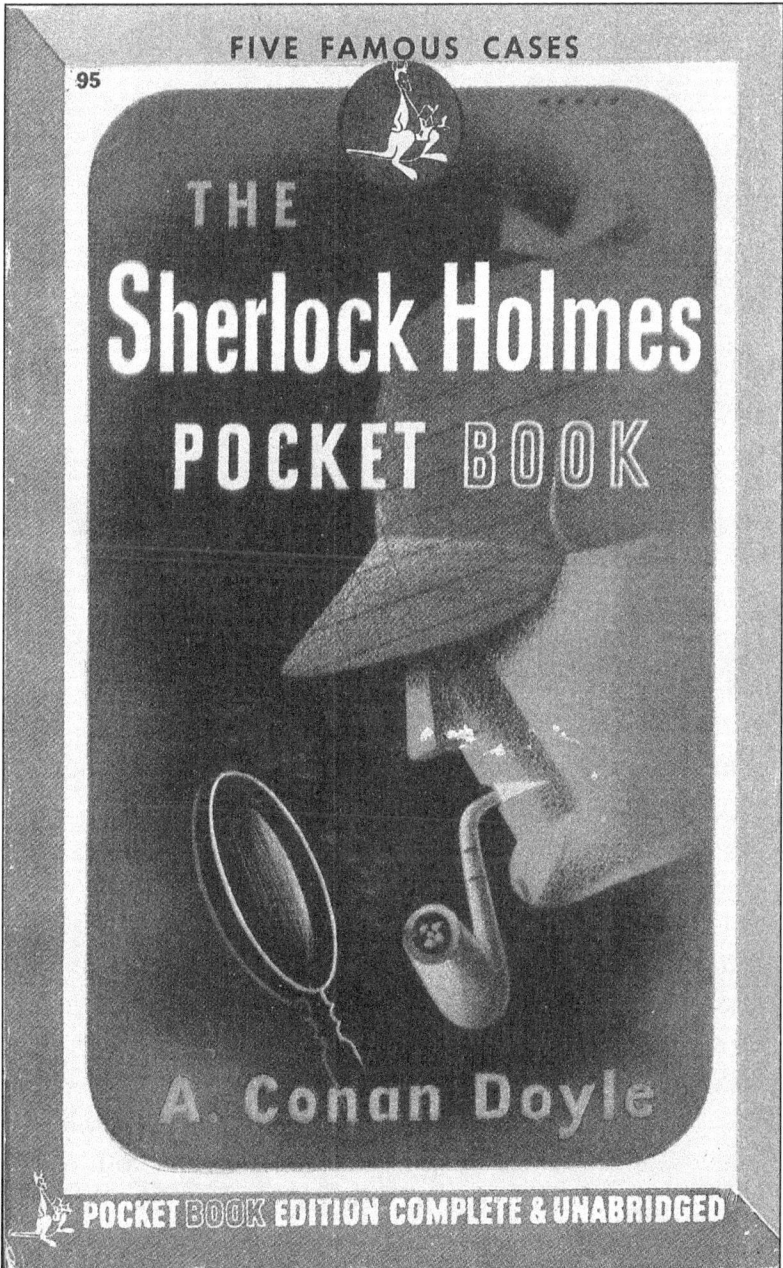

FIVE FAMOUS CASES

95

THE

Sherlock Holmes

POCKET BOOK

A. Conan Doyle

POCKET BOOK EDITION COMPLETE & UNABRIDGED

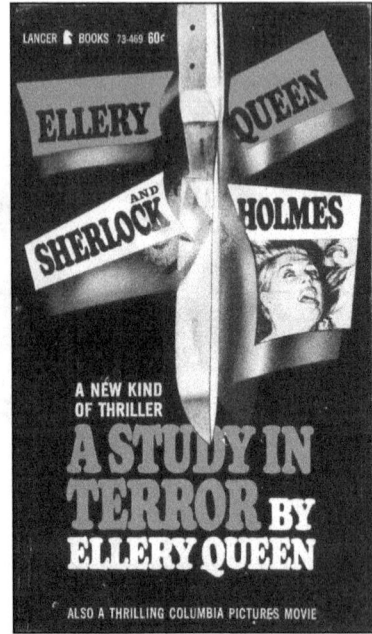

Darkwater Hall Mystery, originally appeared in *Playboy*, May, 1978. It was reprinted in 1978 in a slim UK paperback of only 165 copies and is quite rare today, copies sell for hundreds of dollars.

Many famous team-ups appear in Sherlockian pastichedom since Meyer began the trend of teaming Holmes with Sigmund Freud in *The Seven Per-Cent Solution*. In one of the rarest and most sought after items, Holmes teams up with British secret agent, James Bond! Donald Stanley's *Holmes Meets 007* (Beaune Press, 1967, UK), is a hand-sewn slim booklet published in only 222 numbered copies. It can run you a few hundred dollars, if you can find a copy!

Meanwhile *Pulptime* by P.H. Cannon (Weirdbook Press, 1984), teamed-up Holmes with real-life horror writer H.P. Lovecraft in a memorable and spooky adventure. You couldn't come up with two more quirky and extreme characters than Holmes and Lovecraft.

Science fiction author Philip Jose Farmer teamed-up Holmes with another popular fictional character; Tarzan of the Apes. *The Adventure of the Peerless Peer*, was originally published in a scarce and limited edition hardcover from The Aspen Press in 1974, but it is the Dell paperback reprint that made this wonderful book easily available to legions of Holmes fans at an affordable price.

Pastiches that tie-in to hit films or have become hit films are always popular. One of the earliest was *A Study in Terror* by Ellery Queens (actually written by Paul W. Fairman), a Lancer Books paperback original from 1966. This is the first and best Holmes vs Jack the Ripper novel, told by Watson and Queen in alternating chapters and made into a pretty good – some might say better – film than the book.

They Might Be Giants by James Goldman (Lancer Books, 1970) is a quirky film starring George C. Scott and Joanne Woodward about a judge who thinks he is Sherlock Holmes. The paperback edition — the only edition — contains stills from the film and reprints the actual film script and is rare.

The Private Life of Sherlock Holmes is a tie-in paperback to the hilarious Billy Wilder film and was written by UK Sherlockians Michael and Mollie Hardwick. It novelized the Wilder and I.A.I. Diamond screenplay and appeared as a paperback original in the UK from Mayflower Books in 1970, and was also a first US edition paperback from Bantam Books also in 1970. The Bantam paperback has the added bonus of cover art by Robert McGinnis from his US poster for the film.

Marvin Kaye, is a man who wears many hats as author and anthologist, and past editor of *Sherlock Holmes Mystery Magazine*. He has also written one notable pastiche, *The Incredible Umbrella* (Dell Books, 1980), a first edition paperback that collects his fine stories featuring the fantastical doings of Professor J. Adrian Fillmore. These were originally written as separate stories and appeared in various SF magazines in the 1970s. It is good to have them all collected here in one volume. Sadly, Marvin passed away in

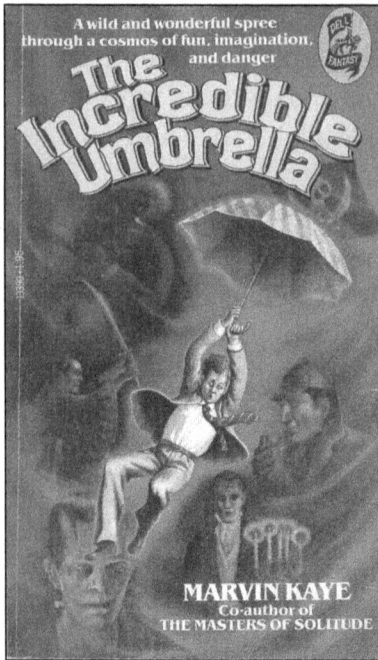

A wild and wonderful spree through a cosmos of fun, imagination, and danger
The Incredible Umbrella
MARVIN KAYE
Co-author of
THE MASTERS OF SOLITUDE

From the original story and screenplay by Billy Wilder and I.A.L. Diamond. Based on the characters created by Sir Arthur Conan Doyle
The Private Life of Sherlock Holmes
A novelization by Michael and Mollie Hardwick

2021.

Kaye is also known for editing three outstanding anthologies of pastiches short stories in the Sherlockian genre. All three were originally published in hardcover by St. Martins Press and then reprinted by them in trade paperback. The first is *The Game is Afoot* (1994), a gem that collects an amazing array of classic and obscure parodies and pastiches together with newer works by popular authors. *Resurrected Holmes* (1996) features all original stories, new cases for which each was ostensibly written by a classic author in that author's style. Thus we have Paula Volsky's "The Giant Rat of Sumatra" as if written by H.P. Lovecraft and Carole Bugge's "The Madness of Colonel Warbutton" as if written by Dashiell Hammett. You get the idea; this one is great fun. *The Confidential Casebook of Sherlock Holmes* (1998) once again offers original pastiches by major authors, this time presenting cases supposedly suppressed to avoid scandal — or worse. Now the truth can be told! In these three books Kaye and his contributors offer some of the most ingenious and enjoyable Sherlockian pastiches.

Carole Bugge, whose fine work appears in this magazine, has also written two excellent novels published by St. Martins Press that you should look for; *The Star of India* (1998) and *The Haunting of Torre Abbey* (2000). In the former we have Holmes returning to London to discover his arch nemesis Moriarty still alive, while the latter has the Great Detective investigating strange hauntings in a 12th Century monastery.

One of the best kept secrets and least known of the newer pastiches *is Sherlock Holmes on The Wild Frontier* by Magda Jozsa (Book Surge, 2005), a print-on-demand trade paperback original from a talented Australian writer. Don't let the American Wild West setting put you off, this is a fine pastiche and true to Holmes and Watson.

While I've barely scratched the surface in this short article, and I'm sure we each have our own favorites, collecting Sherlockian paperbacks is fascinating fun – and you never know what you might discover!

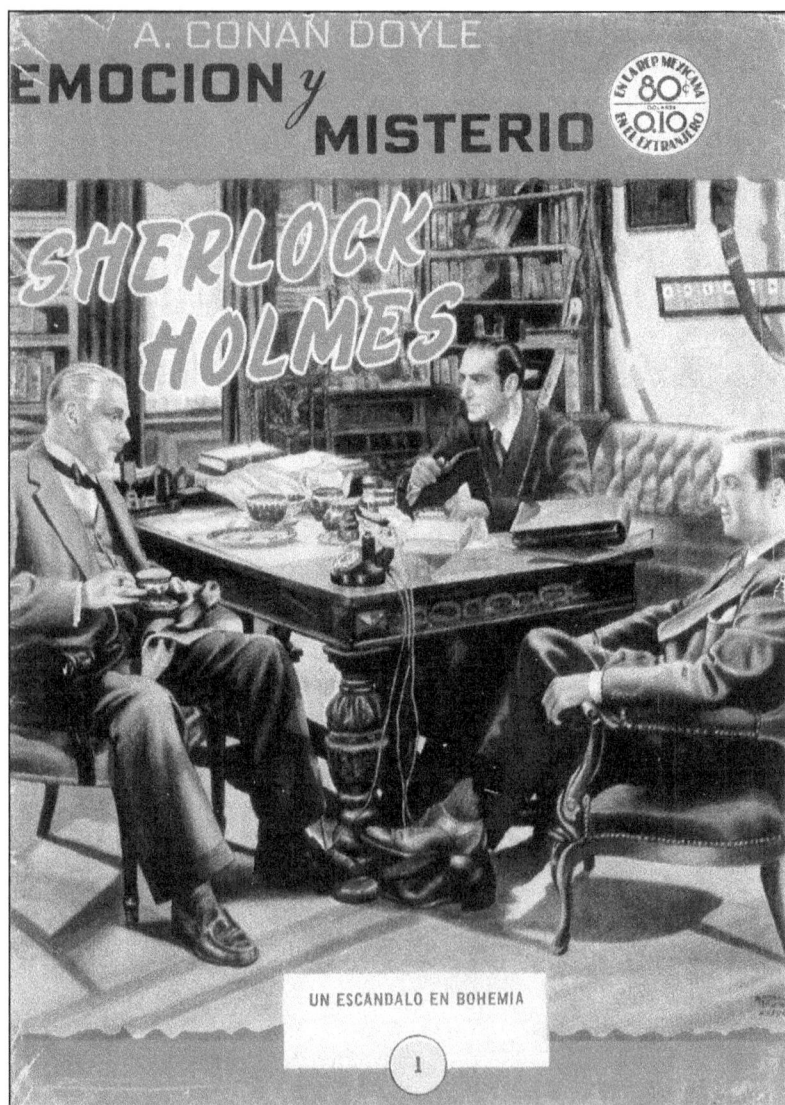

The Rare Mexican
Sherlock Holmes Series

As aficionados of Sherlock Holmes and Doctor Watson we often hurl our nets wide and deep when seeking interesting and sometimes, off-beat items containing our heroes. One of these is the unique and fascinating group of Mexican magazines in the "Emocion Y Misterio Sherlock Holmes" series published by Editorial Olimpo in Mexico City beginning in 1952.

This numbered series was published each week (later, every two weeks), in uniform slim 32-page issues, measuring 9" tall and 6.5" wide. Beginning with issue #1, dated September 5, 1952, containing "Un Escandalo en Bohemia" (I'll allow you to surmise just what Doyle Holmes story that might be), and running to issue #24 in 1953, each issue reprinted one of Doyle's famed Sherlock Holmes short stories translated into Spanish.

The Spanish titles are interesting and often intriguing, some of which such as the example cited above are obvious to Holmes fans even if you have no knowledge of the Spanish language. Other titles may not be so clear as to their original English title. For instance, issue #6, dated November 30, 1952 features "El Hombre Del Labio Leporino" (aka, "The Man With The Twisted Lip").

Issue #24, from 1953, includes a back cover ad that lists all issues and titles published up to that point, but also notes that two further issues (#25 and 26) are "en preparacion." as the Spanish translation informs us. So there may be 26 issues, or more. An extensive Internet search confirmed by my 35 years of collecting Sherlockian items where I have

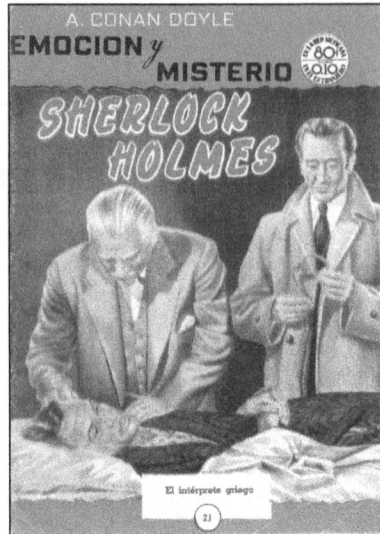

never run across this series, leads me to assume they are fairly rare. Certainly they are rare in the US. A Google search showed none available even among Spanish-language websites.

"Emocion Y Misterio Sherlock Holmes" is actually comprised of two series. The first series contains issues #1 to #20. The second series begins with issue #21 and runs to #24 (or perhaps #26, or later). Perhaps they published the first 20 issues, waited to see how they sold, then published more issues? I am not sure if any issues appeared after #24.

However, the truly magical thing about these lovely little Holmes publications for collectors and fans is the gorgeous cover art. Each issue features a bright, full-color painting showing a key scene from the story with most of them showing Holmes and Watson — using the glorious and iconic images of Basil Rathbone and Nigel Bruce. These are fun cover illustrations with some images seemingly taken directly from Rathbone and Bruce just as they appeared in the classic Universal films of the 1940s. None of this cover art is credited but a barely identifiable signature is visible on some of the covers and appears to be "Mfoms Estuo" (or

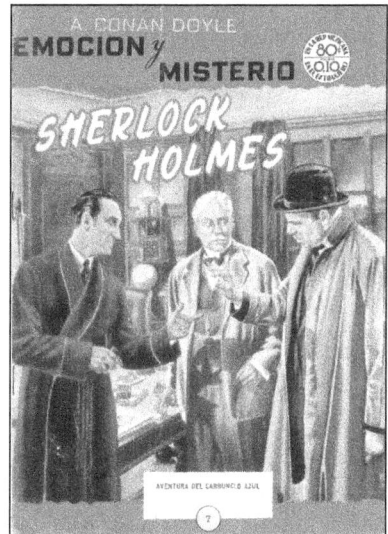

something similar), later shortened to simply "MF". Who this mysterious artist might be, I can not say but he did some very nice renditions of Rathbone and Bruce as our stalwart heroes.

Some of the covers are just stunning. The one for "A Scandal in Bohemia" shows the Rathbone Holmes and the Bruce Watson with a guest in their Baker Street sitting room. We see Holmes seated behind a table piled with papers, with his pipe in hand, while across from him Watson is drinking a cup of tea as they listen to their visitor relate the facts of his case. It's a nice and iconic scene.

Other covers offer up images just as interesting. On issue #7, "Aventura Del Carbunclo Azul" (aka "The Adventure of the Blue Carbuncle") we see Holmes and Watson shown with Inspector Lestrade (which uses the image of Dennis Hoey, the actor who played the Scotland Yard detective in many of the Universal films).

Issue #14, "El Rostro Armarillo" from March 20, 1953, (aka "The Yellow Face"), we see that classic Basil Rathbone profile on the cover that works so well depicting the Great Detective we all know and love.

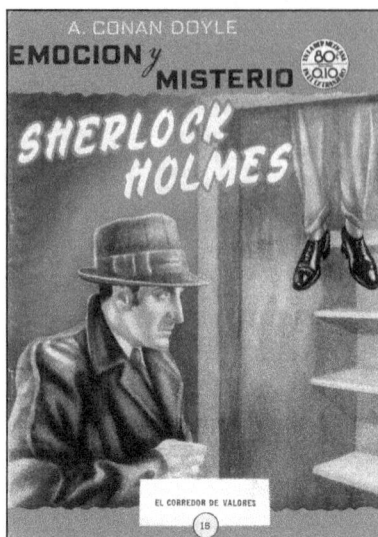

In issue #24, "La Casa Vacia" (aka "The Adventure of the Empty House") we see Holmes and Watson apprehending Professor Moriarty's chief henchman, Colonel Sebastian Moran (the image of Moran is that of actor Alan Mowbray, who played him in the 1946 Universal film, *Terror By Night*).

While the foreign language aspect of this series may make it a bit off-trail for some Holmes buffs, it is a truly lovely and rare series featuring vibrant cover art depicting two of our most popular, best-loved and iconic Holmes and Watson images — Basil Rathbone and Nigel Bruce. It also ties-in nicely with the classic Universal Sherlock Holmes films. For those reasons alone, this series should be treasured and enjoyed. It offers us a glorious collection of rare Sherlock Holmes cover images never seen by most fans and collectors who love everything Holmes and Watson.

These surely are *publicados fantasticos!*

Here are the 24 published editions and two others. How many of the original Doyle titles can you identify?

1. Un escandalo en Bohemia, Sept. 5, 1952
2. La Liga de las Pelirrojos
3. Las Cinco pepitas de Naranja
4. El Misterio del Valle de Boscombe\
5. Un Caso de indentidad
6. El hombre del labio Leporino
7. Aventura del carbunclo azul
8. Aventura de la banda atigeniero
9. Aventura del pulgar del ingeniero
10. Aventura del noble soltero
11. Aventura de la diadema de berilos
12. Aventura de las Hayas Cobrizas
13. "Silver Blaze"
14. El rostro Amarillo
15. El corredor de valores
16. El "Gloria Scott"
17. El ritual de las Musgrave
18. El Enigma de Reigate
19. El lisiado
20. El paciente
21. El interprete griego
22. El pacto naval
23. El problema final
24. La casa vacia

Listed as "En Preparacion"

25. La Aventura del constructor de Norwood
26. La aventura de los munecos bailarines.

[I would like to thank friend and fellow book collector Bruce Edwards for turning me onto these fascinating books.]

Sherlock Holmes & The Case of The German Serials

T he strange case I am about to relate to you gentle reader began in the last days of a cold December morning in the year of '09 — that is — in the year 2009!

That was when my young and lovely wife, Lucille, presented me with a rather odd and certainly unique Sherlockian book as a Christmas gift. She knows I am enamored of nearly everything pertaining to Holmes, no matter how odd or scarce, and this book certainly fit the bill. However, what I did not know at the time was that this book would lead to my discovery of an entire realm of hitherto unknown to me Holmes books — which I now seek to share with you.

The large hardcover book was simply titled "Sherlock Holmes" embossed in gold leaf with the mysterious initials "V.B." in the lower right corner, the only other information on the otherwise dark green simulated green leather hardcover binding. There was no jacket. However as intriguing as the title and mysterious initials were upon the cover of this ancient tome (I guess I should mention now that the book is from 1907 and well over 100 years old!) — what was inside I found much more fascinating.

The book contained 12 individual Sherlock Holmes German dime novel type serials from 1907, bound together. I had never seen their like before but I was instantly fascinated by them, and excited to find out more about them. It was not easy. The text was written in German, and I do not speak or understand the German language. However some information was discernable from simple Holmesian

„Ein geheimnisvoller Schurke sendet mir sein Opfer in einem Koffer in mein Haus. Er will mich damit verhöhnen; doch wir wollen sehen, wer von uns beiden das letzte Wort behält!" rief Sherlock Holmes

observation, so I put the Master's techniques to use to garner
what facts I could.

  This is a series of German dime novel type booklets
entitled *Detektiv Sherlock Holmes und Seine Weltbreuhmten
Abventeur* — which roughly translates into English as
"Sherlock Holmes Most Famous Cases" — though another
translation has it as "Detective Sherlock Holmes and His
World-Famous Adventures". Issue #1 is dated January 2,
1907 and is entitled *Das Geheimnis Jurgen Witwe* — or
"The Mystery of the Young Widow". Each 32-page issue sold
for 20 pfenning, measured roughly 8.5 x 10.5 inches, or
quarto size, and were published weekly in Germany. The
covers featured really wonderful full color illustrations,
many depicting Holmes and his 'companion' (more on this

Der Welt-Detektiv hatte blitzschnell die Füße des Mörders mit einer stählernen Fessel verkettet, dann sprang er ihm von hinten an den Hals und umklammerte diesen mit eisernem Griff.

soon). There is also a small cover box with an illustration of the profile of the Great Detective smoking his ever present pipe looking on in serious deductive thought.

The color cover art for these booklets is just terrific. Issue #1 shows an unmistakable Holmes in the sitting room at 221B standing before a solider and his wife giving his deduction to their problem with his usual aplomb. A traditional image of what appears to be Dr. Watson is seated behind him at a desk.

Issue #4 shows Holmes with a revolver, shocked as he grabs at a criminal's arm — only to discover it detached from the man's body, it is a prosthetic.

Issue #8 shows a startled and weeping woman, whom having removed a painting from where it was hanging upon

Ein teuflisches Lachen erscholl von der Tür her — ein Schuß krachte; im nächsten Moment war der Verbrecher verschwunden.

the wall, reveals a hidden skeleton! It is most effective, as are many of the other covers in this series.

As I did more research on this lovely and fascinating book I began to discern more interesting facts about the series and the stories themselves. The most interesting being that the 12 stories I had in my book (all written in German, in a heavy Gothic font reminiscent of pre-World War I type), were not only all Sherlock Holmes stories — but *none* of them seemed to be Doyle stories! Even though my knowledge of the German language is severely limited I was able to discover this by going through the text of each story line-by-line looking for familiar names from The Canon. I found none. These are, in fact, all new Holmes tales. What I had found were original stories featuring an entirely new set of

„Nein, fie wird nicht Zeugnis geben", fchrie der Verbrecher, der blitzfchnell einen Revolver aus der Tafche geriffen hatte und die Mündung der Waffe an die Schläfe der auffchreienden Naoma richtete.

characters who had come to Holmes with new cases for him
to solve — none of which were created by Doyle!

Even more startling to me was the discovery that while
Holmes was indeed present in every story in dialog and in
quotations, I could not find hide nor hair of his trusty
companion, Dr. John H. Watson. Watson, it seemed did not
exist in these stories at all! I was astounded. Then who was
telling the stories? Well, I soon discovered that the narrator
to these 12 tales was an apparently new companion and
chronicler of the Great Detective — and that was the young
and dashing Harry Taron — in some incarnations called
"Taxson", though the name is difficult for me to make out in
the old Gothic German script. Taron is noted in the text as
der famulus von Sherlock Holmes — or "the friend of

Sherlock Holmes". So, bye-bye Watson! Hello Harry! There is even a drawing of Harry on the first page of the third issue from January 30, 1907, for the story titled *Das Ratfel am Spieltifche*. He looks nothing like Watson at all.

There are in fact, two series, where a new one continues after the first. After issue #10, the series suddenly takes on a new title and drops the name "Sherlock Holmes". I wondered why? Well, it seems that by issue #10 there was some concern (some researchers even call it wrath) by the lawyers for Sir Arthur Conan Doyle that the name of Sherlock Holmes was used in this series, so it was taken out

of the title from issue #11 on.

The new title of the series became *Ausdem Geheimakter des Weltdetektius* or "The Secret Files of The King of Detectives". Nevertheless, while the name of the Great Detective was deleted from the

title of the series, nor was the name of Holmes used in the titles of any of the individual stories, he is unabashedly present under his true name in *every* story — along with his faithful companion and chronicler — Harry Taron!

The series was published by Verlagshaus fur Volksliteratur und Kunst (The Publishing House for Popular Fiction and Art), in Berlin. They had been successful with publishing *groschenromane*, the German equivalent of the dime novel (or penny dreadful). I was further interested to discover that those first issues were noted in English as being published

„Allmächtiger Himmel, was bedeutet das?" fchrie Lady Lifenoß auf und fank halb ohnmächtig in die Knie, während fie entfegt auf das Skelett hinter dem herabgeriffenen Bilde ftarrte. „Habe ich da das Geheimnis eines Mordes entdeckt?"

under "privilege of copyright in the United States of America reserved under the Act approved March 3, 1905". I believe that this means the German publisher contracted with and bought the rights to the character from the American reprinter of Sherlock Holmes, *not* from Doyle and his British publisher. I think that is the reason for the problem with Doyle's lawyers (Doyle was after all alive at this time and still writing his own new Holmes tales), so his lawyers insisted the title of this German series be changed. It was. Though of course the German publisher never eliminated Sherlock Holmes from any of the stories. A rather neat trick of copyright infringement. In fact, during this era, Doyle's Sherlock Holmes appeared in quite a few so-called "pirates", or pirated book editions in America and other countries

Der Capitano und die junge Witwe wollten emporfahren, aber beide blieben auf den Zauberfesseln wie angenagelt sitzen. „Gebt Euch keineMühe, das ist nur ein wenig Elektrizität", rief Sherlock Holmes dem betrügerischen Paare zu.

where Doyle received no payment. I can only imagine Sir Arthur's frustration, and the fact that his solicitor must of had a full-time job insisting upon the protection of Doyle's literary rights, as well as payment for the use of his creation or for reprinting stories in those long ago days before international copyrights, and almost a century before Holmes would legitimately enter the public domain.

As I continued my investigation into this amazing area of Germanic Holmesia, I made use of various helpful sources on the Internet that really opened my eyes to what had gone on here regarding this early unauthorized version of Sherlock Holmes in Europe. This is being done, you must remember, all while Doyle was still alive and it must have been a constant source of irritation to him.

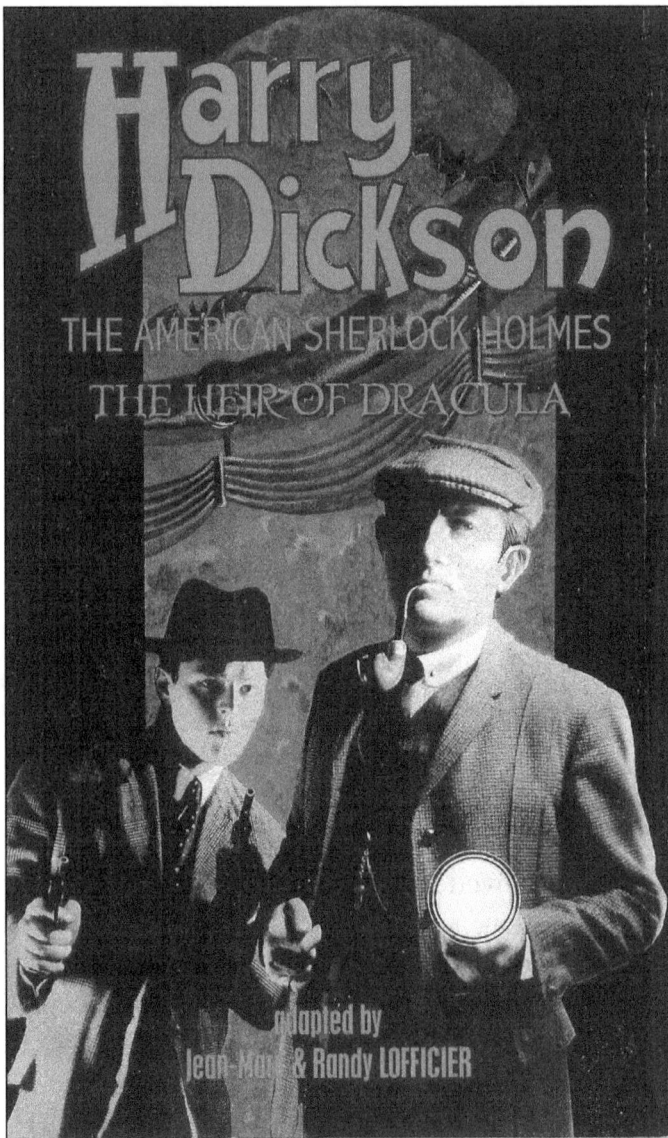

What I discovered next shocked and surprised even myself. For I soon learned that my copies of the first 12 issues of the rare booklets in my hardcover book were only the tip of the iceberg of this strange story. For with booklets apparently being published each week from January, 1907 until June, 1911 — I discovered there were an amazing *230* issues in this series! Truly an incredible accomplishment. Each 32-page issue features a *new* Sherlock Holmes and Harry Taron mystery adventure with a wonderful color cover drawing depicting a key scene from the story. For instance, issue #36 shows a dockyard scene as one man attacks another with a revolver — perhaps Holmes in disguise arresting a villain? While on issue #41 we see Holmes versus a ghastly ghostly

Er fuchte emfig darauf, aber, wie es fchien, ohne olg.

"Harry, wenn du ein tüchtiger Detektiv werden

Harry Taxon, der Famulus von Sherlock Holmes.

illft," rief Sherlock Holmes, indem er feine einfache rawatte vor dem Spiegel knotete, "fo mußt du vor lem ein guter Geograph werden.

image. There are many more covers and all the art is interesting and exciting. Even if you can not read the German stories, these books can be enjoyed for the cover art alone. The main character in all issues of the series is undoubtedly Sherlock Holmes, who is still the solver of amazing crimes and investigates problems that the police can not crack.

It's an intriguing series for any Holmes fan or the lover of pastiche, and while these stories have lately been reprinted by Doyle's German publisher into a series of 34 best-selling paperbacks, I do not believe they have ever appeared in English. That is a shame. I would really love to have the opportunity to read one of these tales in English to see how these early German writers treated the Great Detective and his cases. However, with a new Holmes story appearing in Germany every week in this series, the German publisher had to have a stable of reliable professional writers always at hand — who also had to write *fast* — able to meet incredibly tight deadlines quickly. Certainly none of them could have been as good as Doyle? Or could they? My assumption is that

with 230 stories written by various writers, they must be of
various quality. However, this series was extremely popular
and lasted five years, so the stories must have had positive
aspects going for them other than merely containing the
character Sherlock Holmes. Whether this is the case or not,
it kind of makes me wonder what it might be like to read one
of them today in English — in a decent translation, of
course.

The strange tale of these German Sherlock Holmes stories
does not stop here. In October of 1907, 16 of the original
German stories were adapted into French by the publisher
Fernand Laven. Later on, in 1927, a Dutch publisher did their
version of the German stories, this time under the title *Harry
Dickson de Amerikaansche Sherlock Holmes* or "Harry
Dickson, the American Sherlock Holmes". Holmes was now
changed to Dickson and now became American! Holmes
remained Dickson from then on. In this new version Holmes
(or I should say, Dickson) still has his assistant, but now the
assistant's name has been changed yet again, now from
Harry Taron to Tom Wills. This Dutch series lasted 180 issues
until May, 1935.

Also in 1928, Belgian publisher Janssens had author Jean
Ray translate the Dutch series into French and the well-
known French-language editions of *Harry Dickson, le
Sherlock Holmes Americain*, began in January, 1929 and ran
178 issues until April, 1938, just before World War II began
and Paris fell. Ray soon began writing original stories
published with cover art supplied by noted German artist
Alfred Roloff. Roloff's excellent artwork is said to have
inspired Ray's desire to write new stories. In France, Harry
Dickson's fame is said to rival that of Arsene Lupin and even
the great Sherlock Holmes himself.

In 2009, Black Coat Press published an attarctive trade
paperback collecting four of these stories from the 1930s in
Harry Dickson, adapted by Jean-Marc and Randy Lofficier.
It has nice cover art by Jean-Michel Nicollet. This book

offers stories from *The Secret Files of The King of Detectives*. It is an intersting Holmes pastiche collection and now we can read them in English translations!

While these various series may be fodder for another day, it is worthy to note that the beginnings of Sherlock Holmes pastiche in Europe began over a hundred years ago in Germany, way back in 1905 with a lovely little series of dime novel booklets — or as I have put it — with Sherlock Holmes and the case of the German serials.

The Ironic Story of
The Stevenson - Doyle Letters

S ynchronicity in discovery can be a wonderful thing.
When I came upon a two-volume set of *The Letters of
Robert Louis Stevenson* I had no idea what gold I would
discover within the 900+ pages — some of it my dear friends,
of a Sherlockian nature! It is not a story of horror, such as
that written by Stevenson in his classic, *Dr. Jekyll & Mr.
Hyde*, but a tale that contains fascinating irony. In fact, it is a
strange and interesting story, yet strikes a sad note about the
wonderful relationship between two of the most famous and
beloved writers of all time. Two men whose works still live
with us today and have stood the test of time.

Letter writing was once the major communication medium
back in the day. When famed author (and creator of
Treasure Island [1883] and *Dr. Jekyll & Mr. Hyde* [1887]
among many others), Robert Louis Stevenson wrote the first
of four letters to Arthur Conan Doyle in 1893, it was because
Stevenson greatly admired Doyle and his work. That feeling
of admiration was very much reciprocated by Sir Arthur.
Doyle admired Stevenson's *Treasure Island* and considered
Dr. Jekyll & Mr. Hyde a masterpiece of Gothic storytelling.

Stevenson's four letters to Doyle appear in a rare two-
volume edition *The Letters of Robert Louis Stevenson* edited
by Sidney Colvin (Charles Scribners Sons, 1901, New York),
the first US edition of Stevenson's letters. These attractive
books are in red cloth binding with gold lettering on cover,
spine and top pages edges. Volume One features letters to
Stevenson's friends and family from his younger days from
1868 to 1885. However, we are concerned with Volume Two,

containing letters from 1886 to 1894, written to such
luminaries as Rudyard Kipling, Henry James, J. M Barrie,
William Morris, Andrew Lang — and his four letters to
Arthur Conan Doyle. While the two volumes contain over
900 pages of Stevenson's letters, editor Sidney Colvin (who
knew the author well) stated that they formed a mere 15-20
percent of Stevenson's overall letters. Interestingly enough, it
seemed Stevenson did
not like writing letters
very much, he considered
himself a bad
correspondent.

In his letters to Doyle,
Stevenson writes of his
recognition of Dr. Joseph
Bell as being the basis for
Sherlock Holmes.
Ironically, it seems the
two authors — both
Scotsmen who lived in
Edinburgh actually knew
Dr. Bell. Even more
ironic, Stevenson
graduated from the University of Edinburgh in 1875, a year
before Doyle enrolled there to study medicine. But the irony
of this tale does not stop there.

Stevenson was a fan of Doyle's Sherlock Holmes stories
and even commented on the Holmes story "The Engineer's
Thumb" in one letter, and on the influence that Doyle had on
his classic novel, *Treasure Island*.

In the book *Arthur Conan Doyle, A Life in Letters*, edited
by Jon Lellenberg, Daniel Stashower and Charles Folly
(Penguin Press, 2007), some of Doyle's letters, most to his
mother, Mary, are published. On page 430, Doyle mentions
the four letters he received from Stevenson, and wrote about
them, "I had the most encouraging letters from him in 1893

Arthur and Innes on their way to America.

and 1894. 'O frolic fellow-spookiest' was Stevenson's curious
term of personal salutation on one of these, which showed
that he shared my interest in psychic research but did not
take it very seriously." In fact, I believe Stevenson was lightly
teasing Doyle about his spiritualist leanings.

However, as I have stated, there was much more.
Stevenson writes about a meeting between the two great
authors. This was a rather difficult accomplishment at the
time, since in 1893-94 — the time Stevenson wrote his four
letters to Doyle — he was living far away in the village of
Vailima, on the Pacific island of Samoa. Doyle was living in
the UK. Almost ten thousand miles separated the two men.
However, by this time Stevenson and Doyle had become
famous authors and also world travelers — so that while
such a meeting might be time-consuming or difficult to
schedule — it was eminently possible. The two men very
much wanted to meet, and the logistics of such a meeting

were mentioned in Stevenson's letters.

In fact, Conan Doyle made definite plans to extend his September, 1894 American Tour. The plan was for him to leave from San Francisco and include a visit to Stevenson in Samoa — where RLS had made his permanent home since 1890.

Stevenson's correspondence to Doyle is fascinating and quite lively. At times whimsical and even poetic. The irony and sadness is what we know about today so many years later, which does not come through in the letters, though Stevenson in his last letter to Doyle does mention his own death.

Now, in his own words, here are Stevenson's four letters to Doyle, and one reply form Doyle that I was able to find. Here is the actual text of the letters:

Letter: to Doyle

VAILIMA, APIA, SAMOA, APRIL 5TH, 1893

DEAR SIR, - You have taken many occasions to make yourself very agreeable to me, for which I might in decency have thanked you earlier. It is now my turn; and I hope you will allow me to offer you my compliments on your very ingenious and very interesting adventures of Sherlock Holmes. That is the class of literature that I like when I have the toothache. As a matter of fact, it was a pleurisy I was enjoying when I took the volume up; and it will interest you as a medical man to know that the cure was for the moment effectual. Only the one thing troubles me: can this be my old friend Joe Bell? - I am, yours very truly,

ROBERT LOUIS STEVENSON

P.S. - And lo, here is your address supplied me here in Samoa! But do not take mine, O frolic fellow Spookist, from the same source; mine is wrong

R.L.S.

Letter: Response from Doyle to Stevenson's April 5, 1893 letter

I'm so glad Sherlock Holmes helped to pass an hour for you. He's a bastard between Joe Bell [a famous Edinburgh surgeon] and Poe's Monsieur Dupin (much diluted). I trust that I may never write a word about him again. I had rather that you knew me by my *White Company*. I'm sending it on the chance that you have not seen it."

Letter: To Doyle

VAILIMA, JULY 12, 1893

MY DEAR DR. CONAN DOYLE — THE WHITE COMPANY has not yet turned up; but when it does - which I suppose will be in next mail - you shall hear news of me. I have a great talent for compliment, accompanied by a hateful, even a diabolic frankness.

Delighted to hear I have a chance of seeing you and Mrs. Doyle; Mrs. Stevenson bids me say (what is too true) that our rations are often spare. Are you Great Eaters? Please reply. As to ways and means, here is what you will have to do. Leave San Francisco by the down mail, get off at Samoa, and twelve days or a fortnight later, you can continue your journey to Auckland per Upolu, which will give you a look at Tonga and possibly Fiji by the way. Make this a FIRST PART OF YOUR PLANS. A fortnight, even of Vailima diet, could kill nobody.

We are in the midst of war here; rather a nasty business, with the head-taking; and there seem signs of other trouble. But I believe you need make no change in your design to visit us. All should be well over; and if it were not, why! You need not leave the steamer — Yours very truly,

ROBERT LOUIS STEVENSON

THE HOUSE AT VAILIMA AFTER THE ADDITIONS.

Letter: To Doyle

VAILIMA, AUGUST 23RD, 1893

MY DEAR DR. CONAN DOYLE, - I am reposing after a somewhat severe experience upon which I think it my duty to report to you. Immediately after dinner this evening it occurred to me to re-narrate to my native overseer Simele your story of THE ENGINEER'S THUMB. And, sir, I have done it. It was necessary, I need hardly say, to go somewhat farther afield than you have done. To explain (for instance) what a railway is, what a steam hammer, what a coach and horse, what coining, what a criminal, and what the police. I pass over other and no less necessary explanations. But I did actually succeed; and if you could have seen the drawn, anxious features and the bright, feverish eyes of Simele, you would have (for the moment at least) tasted glory. You might perhaps think that, were you to come to Samoa, you might be introduced as the Author of THE ENGINEER'S THUMB. Disabuse yourself. They do not know what it is to make up a story. THE ENGINEER'S THUMB (God forgive me) was narrated as a piece of actual and factual history. Nay, and more, I who write to you have had the indiscretion to perpetrate a trifling piece of fiction entitled THE BOTTLE

IMP. Parties who come up to visit my unpretentious
mansion, after having admired the ceilings by Vanderputty
and the tapestry by Gobbling, manifest towards the end a
certain uneasiness which proves them to be fellows of an
infinite delicacy. They may be seen to shrug a brown
shoulder, to roll up a speaking eye, and at last secret burst
from them: 'Where is the bottle?' Alas, my friends (I feel
tempted to say), you will find it by the Engineer's Thumb!
Talofa-soifuia.

Oa'u, O lau no moni, O Tusitala.

More commonly known as,

R.L. STEVENSON.

Have read the REFUGEES; Conde and old P. Murat very
good; Louis XIV and Louvois with the letter bag very rich.
You have reached a trifle wise perhaps; too MANY
celebrities? Though I was delighted to re-encounter my old
friend Du Chaylu. Old Murat is perhaps your high water
mark; 'tis excellently human, cheerful and real. Do it again.
Madame de Maintenon struck me as quite good. Have you
any document for the decapitation? It sounds steepish. The
devil of all that first part is that you see old Dumas; yet your
Louis XIV is DISTINCTLY GOOD. I am much interested with
this book, which fulfills a good deal, and promises more.
Question: How far a Historical Novel should be wholly
episodic? I incline to that view, with trembling. I shake hands
with you on old Murat.

R.L.S.

Letter: To Doyle.

[This letter refers to articles by various authors in the
magazine, *Idler*, under the title "My First Book".]

VAILIMA, SAMOA, SEPTEMBER 9, 1894

MY DEAR CONAN DOYLE, - If you found anything to
entertain you in my TREASURE ISLAND article, it may
amuse you to know that you owe it entirely to yourself.
YOUR 'First Book' was by some accident read aloud one

"THE PLAZA" (PORTSMOUTH SQUARE).

THE FAVOURITE LOUNGING-PLACE OF ROBERT LOUIS STEVENSON IN SAN FRANCISCO,
WITH THE MEMORIAL TO HIM DESIGNED BY BRUCE PORTER AND WILLIS POLK.

night in my Baronial 'All. I was consumedly amused by it, so
was the whole family, and we proceeded to hunt up back
IDLERS and read the whole series. It is a rattling good series,
even people whom you would not expect came in quite the
proper tone - Miss Braddon, for instance, who was really one
of the best where all are good - or all but one! …in short, I
fell in love with 'The First Book' series, and determined that

it should be all our first books, and that I could not hold back where the white plume of Conan Doyle waved gallantly in the front. I hope they will republish them, though it's a grievous thought to me that that effigy in the German cap - likewise the other effigy of the noisome old man with the long hair, telling indelicate stories to a couple of deformed negresses in a rancid shanty full of wreckage - should be perpetuated. I may seem to speak in pleasantry - it is only a seeming - that German cap, sir, would be found, when I come to die, imprinted on my heart. Enough - my heart is too full. Adieu. - Yours very truly,
   ROBERT LOUIS STEVENSON

Alas, with plans set and both men willing, the greatest irony of all is that these two giants of popular fiction would never meet. The most ironic event of all — obviously instituted by the Fates themselves — in the same month that Conan Doyle killed off Sherlock Holmes at the Reichenbach Falls — Robert Louis Stevenson suffered a brain hemorrhage and died in his beloved Samoa. He was only 44 years old.

References:

The Letters of Robert Louis Stevenson Volume 1 and 2, edited by Sidney Colvin, Charles Scribners Sone, 1901, New York. Stevenson photos are reproduced from these editions.

Arthur Conan Doyle, A Life in Letters edited by Jon Lellenberg, Danial Stashower and Charles Foley, Penguin Press, 2007.

"Dr. Doyle and Mr. Stevenson" by Mark Shanahan, Alley Theater website

"Robert Louis Stevenson's Letters to Doyle 1893-4" in *Markings*, internet, no author listed, June 21, 2012.

Sherlock Holmes — in The Cards

O ver the last few years it has been my pleasure to share various Sherlock Holmes items with the readers of *Sherlock Holmes Mystery Magazine*. As a collector and author it is a pleasure to pass on information about unique and fascinating items of Sherlockania. Of course we all know the world of Holmes and Watson is not just limited to stories or books — nor films, magazines, or even comic books — but to a plethora of more esoteric items. Some of them are quite interesting and often rare collectables.

A good example of this is the British Turf Cigarette set of 25 cards which were published by Alexander Boguslavsky, Ltd., 55 Piccadilly, London, in 1923. This set of charming antique picture cards is officially named the "Conan Doyle Characters" set, but it might as well have been called the Sherlock Holmes and characters card set because Holmes, or characters from The Canon, are featured on 19 of the 25 cards. The six exceptions being cards for characters that appear in

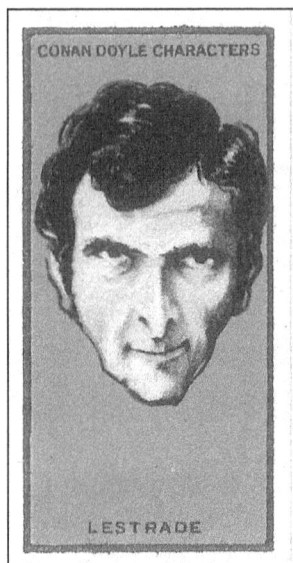

Doyle's historical novels. The rest of the cards feature nice color drawings of Sherlock Holmes (with pipe, and another card of him in disguise), also Watson, Moriarty, Lestrade, Irene Adler, Tonga, Miss Mary Morstan, and many famous characters found in the Holmes stories. The only non-human character card is the hound from *The Hound of The Baskervilles.* The artist is unknown and the art is nice and colorful and gives us tight head shots of each character in the style of cigarette card art of the era.

The Turf Cigarette Cards measure 1 3/8 x 2 5/8 inches in size — the standard size for antique cigarette cards, with one card being included in each pack of Turf Cigarettes. Each card is numbered, and of course card #1 is Sherlock Holmes, and card #2 is Holmes in disguise. I assume the card series was authorized by Doyle, who was alive at the time. I also assume that he did not want it to be a Holmes cards series — so it was officially named the Conan Doyle Characters card series and Turf added six other non-Holmes characters. Doyle was particularly proud of his historical novels, and so the addition of a Sir Nigel Loring card and a Brigadier Gerard card, among four others, may have met with his approval of the series. Turf didn't always get prior approval for their cigarette cards (i.e. Honus Wagner), however, if permissions were needed, I am sure

Doyle would have balked at a card series featuring Holmes and Canonical characters exclusively.

The back of each card has a two or three paragraph description of that character, while the single-story character cards also list the story that character appears in. There seem to be two sets of these cards, one with a green print back and one with a black print back, but I do not know if the color of ink makes one card a first printing or not — it seems not to matter. Any of these cards of any type are scarce. What does matter is the front cover art showing each character, and what is written on the backs of these cards about that character. The back of card #1 picturing Sherlock Holmes describes the Great Detective thusly:

The nature of a detective's work makes it essential that he should avoid publicity. Perhaps that is why no "real life" detective has won the notoriety of Sherlock Holmes, the hero of so many of Sir Arthur Conan Doyle's tales.
One cannot help wondering, however, if there exists, outside the pages of history, anyone quite so clever at unraveling mysteries as this remarkable man, with his ingenious methods of work and extraordinary powers of observation.

The above paragraph must have been written before it was

generally known that Dr. Joseph Bell was the template Doyle used for Holmes.

The back of card #2 titled "Sherlock Holmes in Disguise" lists him this way:

Besides hoodwinking criminals whom he wished to track, Sherlock Holmes used to get fun out of the way in which his disguises deceived even his intimate friends.

In "The Sign of Four" he appeared as "an aged man, clad in seafaring garb, with an old peajacket buttoned up to his throat," and until he resumed his natural voice Dr. Watson had no suspicion that he was anything but "a respectable master mariner who had fallen into years and poverty."

Card #3 features Dr. Watson, and it describes him in this manner:

Dr. Watson, Sherlock Holmes' friend, often appears unobservant, and even a little stupid, in contrast with the famous detective. Those who are inclined to despise him, however, should try their own hand at playing the part of Sherlock Holmes and learn humility!

Holmes was lucky in having a friend who was willing to play second fiddle, yet always ready with his help when required, even if he knew it meant risking his life.

I do not agree with all of the above. Watson was a medical doctor and not "stupid" and I certainly cannot believe there are any Holmes fans who actually "despise" Watson — quite the opposite, but that is the description given on the back of his card.

Other character cards offer further interesting descriptions. Card #7, Professor Moriarty tells us:

Professor Moriarty was Sherlock Holmes' arch-enemy, whom the latter once described as "the Napoleon of crime" and recognized as his intellectual equal.

A life-and-death struggle between the two men took place on the edge of a precipice, and in order to mislead the members of Dr. Moriarty's gang who were seeking his life, Sherlock Holmes let people go on for several years thinking that he, as well as his enemy, had been killed.

In the above "Dr." Moriarty is not a typo of mine — perhaps the card writer confused the Professor with Watson's medical title? Another important character in The Canon is Irene Adler, and her card (#22) describes her thusly:

To Sherlock Holmes, Irene Adler was always "the woman" — not because he had fallen in love with her — that emotion being "abhorrent to his cold, precise, but admirably balanced mind" — but because she had seen through his plan of campaign and frustrated it.
After meeting this woman whose brains were a match for his own, we are told that Sherlock Holmes ceased to make merry over the cleverness of women."

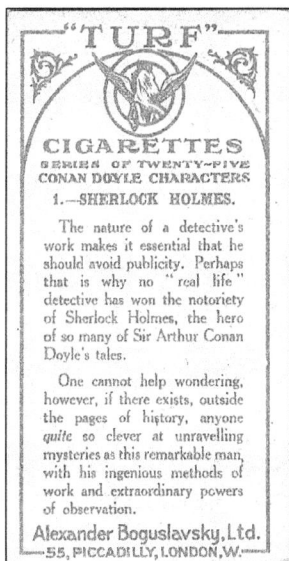

These short back-of-the-card descriptions add to the charm of these cards and I believe they must have been useful to readers who may not have been familiar with all the Holmes stories, or Doyle's other books. They add an important perspective to the character images and the cards themselves.

One note to collectors, all 25 cards are shown in black and white on page 9 of *The Sherlock Holmes Scrapbook* edited by Peter Haining, many are also shown in color throughout the pages of *The Sherlock Holmes Companion* by Daniel Smith, and the entire 19 canonical set is shown in color on page 70 in *Sherlock Holmes: A Centeneary Celebration* by Allen Eyles..

Below is a complete list of the 1923 British Turf Cigarette Card Set:

#1: Sherlock Holmes

#2: Sherlock Holmes in Disguise

#3: Dr. Watson

#4: Lestrade

#5: Miss Mary Morstan, from "The Sign of Four"

#6: Tonga, from "The Sign of Four"

#7: Professor Moriarty, from *Memoirs of Sherlock Holmes.*

#8: Lucy Ferrier, from "A Study in Scarlet"

#9: Jefferson Hope, from "A Study in Scarlet"

#10: Dame Ermyntrude Loring, from *Sir Nigel.*

#11: Sir Nigel Loring, from *Sir Nigel* and *The White Company.*

#12: Miss Helen Stoner, from "The Speckled Band"

#13: Dr. Grimsby Roylette, from "The Speckled Band"

#14: Mother Superior, from *Adventures of Gerard.*

#15: Brigadier Gerard, from *Adventures of Gerard.*

#16: The hound of the Baskervilles, from *The Hound of the Baskervilles.*

#17: Miss Stapleton, from *The House of The Baskervilles.*

#18: "The Man with the Twisted Lip" from *Adventures of Sherlock Holmes.*

#19: Holly Hinton, from *Rodney Stone.*

#20: The King of Bohemia, from "A Scandal in Bohemia"

#21: Mr. Jabez Wilson, from "The Red-Headed League"

#22: Irene Adler, from "A Scandal in Bohemia"

#23: Miss Violet Hunter, from "The Copper Beeches"
#24: Rebecca Tayforth, from *The Firm of Gridlestone.*
#25: Miss Hatty Doran, from "The Noble Bachelor"

These lovely little British Turf Cigarette cards can be great fun to collect but finding them all can be a real challenge to even the most die-hard Sherlockian. First published in 1923, these pretty little cigarette cards are now almost a hundred years old, so they have become quite rare. While some cards may be more common than others, all are difficult to find, especially in nice condition, but they are certainly worth the search for any fan and collector. And who knows — using methods developed by the Great Detective — you may even find some of these little gems. I am sure you will enjoy them.

The Adventure of
The Sherlock Holmes Chocolate Cards

Following in the footsteps of The Great Detective, many of us seek out the more outré aspects of being a Sherlock Holmes fan by collecting unusual items relating to our hero. In doing so, it is possible to find odd items relating to him that are fascinating, often rare, but again always fun. Some of the best of these are the picture cards that were done for an obscure and long-forgotten chocolate maker in Barcelona, Spain, over eight decades ago!

Now there are a lot of Holmes related picture cards out there. Going way back to the early 20th Century there were many Sherlock Holmes cigarette picture cards and series. These were small cards included free inside cigarette packages of the era. There are various sets of these, mostly from the UK, such as the Turf card series, and all are avidly collected.

However, just as desirable, and even more rare, is the generally unknown series of known as the "Chocolate Jaime Boix" cards. These are not cigarette cards, but are what are termed "trade cards", printed for business advertising. These cards are larger than cigarette cards, roughly being the size of a standard postal card, and they feature a color illustration from a story of the canon on one side, with text in Spanish about the illustration and story, on the other side — along with advertising information that gives the chocolate maker's name and address in Barcelona.

These cards are quite simply a lovely group of Sherlock Holmes illustrated images. The cards comprise three series that total 40 cards, none are dated but they are from the 1930s.

Aventuras de Sherlock Holmes
Série A.—Núm. 2
EL RITUAL DE LOS MUSGRAVE

Series A tells the story of "The Musgrave Ritual" ("El Ritual de los Musgrave" from *The Adventures of Sherlock Holmes*), in ten cards, numbered 1 to 10.

Series B recounts "The Speckled Band" ("La Banda Moteada"), with ten cards numbered 11 to 20.

Series C tells the tale of *The Sign of The Four* ("La Marca de los Cuarto"), this time taking 20 cards to illustrate the story, cards numbered 21 to 40.

El Ritual de los Musgrave
Série A.—Núm. 3

Una tarde de invierno,...

El Ritual de los Musgrave
Série A.—Núm. 4

—Necesito vuestra ayuda...

El Ritual de los Musgrave
Série A.—Núm. 10

Aquí tenéis la corona...

La Banda Moteada
Série B.—Núm. 16

Y cogiendo las tenazas de la chimenea...

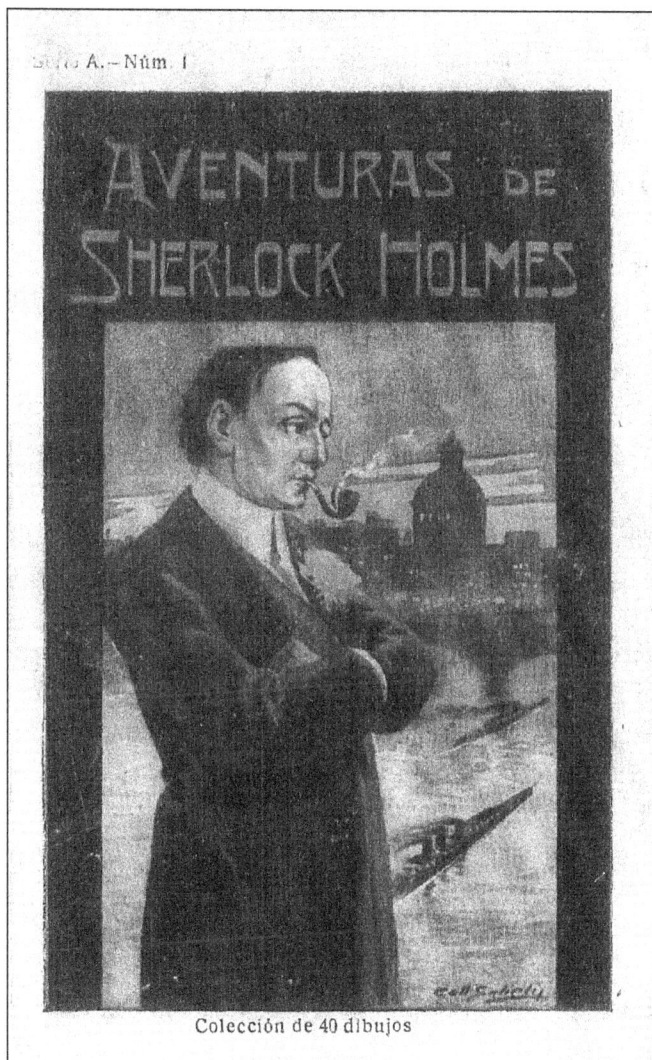

Serie A.–Núm. 1

AVENTURAS DE SHERLOCK HOLMES

Colección de 40 dibujos

The first card in each of these three series is a charming title card, featuring the name of the Holmes adventure and a design and illustration that captures some aspect of that particular story. The exception is the Series A #1 card, which is the first card in the set, which acts as a title card for the entire set. It is titled "Aventuras de Sherlock Holmes" and has an excellent image of Holmes with arms crossed, pipe in mouth, looking thoughtful as his eyes gaze over his London domain. Quite impressive. The rest of the cards offer terrific artwork depicting Holmes and Watson, along with various characters and villains from the three stories.

The art on cards 2, 7 and 8 of "The Musgrave Ritual" offer us stark images of murder as Holmes and Watson find a body while they investigate the Musgrave estate. Card 21, the title card for "The Sign of The Four" shows some of the stolen treasure behind this dark case. Cards 16 and 17 for "The Speckled Band" feature images of Holmes and Watson with an agitated and most deadly villainous Dr. Roylott, and in the latter card, with a pensive Miss Stoner.

The art on all these cards is quite good, and while the artist is unknown — the art *is* signed but it is difficult to make out the artist's name — which appears to be something like "cell Soliolifoto." The art is reminiscent of that seen on the covers of dime novels of the early 20th Century, a bit more formal than we are used to today, but it offers a view into a past world that now is long gone. Regardless, the images are bright and colorful, accurate to the canon and full of suspense and wonder — which is just the way we love to see our Sherlock Holmes and his trusty Watson.

These cards are incredibly rare, and a set of all 40 cards is virtually impossible to obtain and would likely cost hundreds of dollars. The individual cards sell for from $10 to $25 depending on condition and the image on the card — obviously cards depicting Holmes and Watson go for a higher price.

As if this series isn't impossible enough to complete, full disclosure forces me to at least mention that there is an even earlier and even more rare series of Spanish chocolate trade cards from the 1920s. The "El Detective Sherlock Holmes" 10 card series put out by Fabrica de Chocolate de Jaime Torras Arano — but we'll leave this one as fodder for another article, on another day.

To sum up, the 1930s Spanish Chocolate Jaime Boix trade card series offers 40 wonderful visions from three classic

La Marca de los Cuatro — Série C.—Núm. 27
... reposaba el cadáver de Bartolomé Sholto ..

La Marca de los Cuatro — Série C.—Núm. 30
... habían diferentes animales...

La Marca de los Cuatro — Série C.—Núm. 32
Obligamos á Toby á husmearlas...

La Marca de los Cuatro — Série C.—Núm. 33
... empezó á tocar una sonata dulce ..

Holmes stories that surely will stimulate any Sherlockian collector's appetite for the rare and obscure relating to The Great Detective. These unusual cards are great fun to collect, but it can be frustrating because they are nearly impossible to find — which is why it is such an adventure to locate them and complete a set — but they are well worth your search. As Holmes himself might tell us, half of the fun is in the hunt. So let the adventure begin!

[I would like to thank Robert C. Hess for his kind assistance with information for this article.]

Sherlockian Connections:
Bodies In A Bookshop

There are many books that pastiche the Great Detective, Sherlock Holmes. Some try to give us an outright mirror-image of Doyle's famed creation — this is not one of those. However in the mood of this story, the tight plotting, and above all in the quirkiness of its well-developed characters seeking to solve a complex and mysterious murder — *Bodies in A Bookshop* by R.T. Campbell should be high upon your must-read list. I am sure it will thrill even the most die-hard Holmes fan and its Sherlockian connections are avid and a real joy. If you have not read it then you should remedy that deficiency at once. I have neglected this book myself, and only ten years ago discovered the gem within, albeit better late than never. Nevertheless, it is a novel that has stood the test of time, a sure-fire neglected mystery classic with some amusing Sherlockian connections.

Bodies In A Bookshop is a fun crime romp; a cutting biblio murder mystery with some truly fascinating characters. The case begins when a bookman named Leslie, and one other fellow named Baird, are found dead in a bookstore. They are found dead apparently via a gas leak in a locked room so the mystery deepens. Was it an accident or murder? Leslie owns the bookstore, and Baird is later discovered to be a blackmailer. From then we are introduced to our brave trio of sleuths, both amateur and professional, who join forces to solve the mystery and eventually discover the killer.

Bodies In A Bookshop was originally published in 1946 in a UK hardcover from John Westhouse, Ltd., but can more

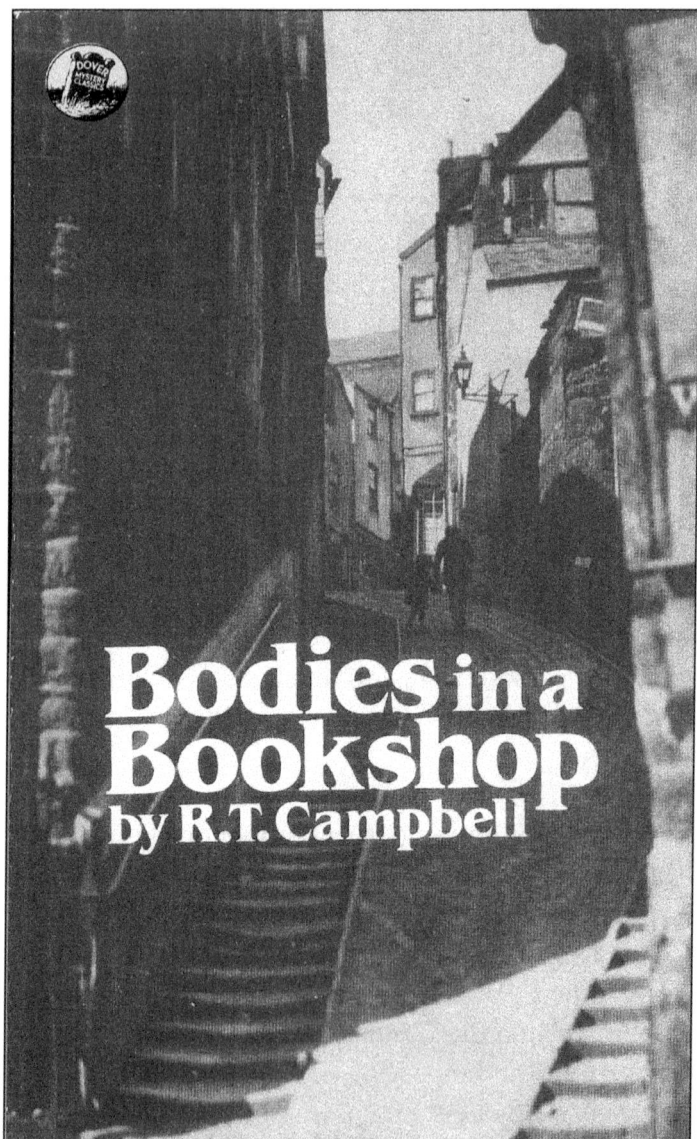

commonly be found today in a slim, inexpensive Dover
Books trade paperback from 1984, the cover price back then
was just $6.95. You can find copies on the Internet for just a
buck or two — a great value and well worth it. The book was
actually written by Scottish-born poet, scholar, art critic and
novelist Ruthven Campbell Todd (1914-1978). He wrote a
series of detective novels using the pen-name R.T. Campbell.
His other crime novel was *Unholy Dying*, also in a Dover
Books trade paperback. I've not read this one yet, but on the
strength of *Bodies In A Bookshop*, it is certainly high on my
'must read list' and I will be on the lookout for any of
Campbell's works now.

   This fine novel opens with some well-known bookish
themes that book lovers and collectors can easily relate to in
any biblio mystery. It also sets the stage for what is to follow
by introducing two of our three sleuths: young Max Boyle,
the narrator, and the irascible but loveable Professor John
Stubbs. From page 7 Max explains:

   *I don't know what came over me. It wasn't as if there were
   not enough books in the house to begin with. There were
   books on the floor, books on all the tables, books on the beds
   — and in the beds if one wasn't careful. Only that morning
   I had removed three volumes of Curtis from my room. How
   they came to be there I would not know. There seems to be a
   plot between the old man, Professor John Stubbs, and his
   housekeeper, Mrs. Farley, to dump anything they like in my
   room. So far as I am concerned that is fine. I like books. I
   like mess. But I have books enough and mess enough of my
   own.*

   From this point on we follow the adventures of an amazing
triumvirate of very British sleuths: the narrator and botanist
Max Boyle; Professor John Stubbs, and Chief Inspector
Reginald "The Bishop" Bishop of Scotland Yard. These three
very individualistic fellows (read: eccentric, though each are

thoroughly delightful in their own way) lead us through a variety of clues in and about the London book world of the late 1940s. The trio has a complex puzzle to solve. It includes investigations into the crimes of "erotic art," book theft, blackmail and other tawdry aspects of the rare book business where serious money is involved. There is also considerable danger.

Max and the Professor are interesting characters who live together much as Holmes and Watson did, and there is much that is Sherlockian in their friendship as they work to solve this crime with their faithful friend from Scotland Yard, The Bishop —a gruffer version of Lestrade. There's constant competition and good-natured bickering between the Proff and The Bishop with Max often playing the referee — or the Watson role between Holmes and Lestrade. You'll get a good dose of their Sherlockian relationship and style of investigation in this brief excerpt from page 135:

The Professor ignored my remarks. He took out his immense flame-throwing petrol-lighter and applied its flare to his pipe. Once he was comfortably surrounded with clouds of nauseous smoke, he leaned back on the bed and grinned at me. He certainly seemed to be very pleased with himself. I scowled at him. I just couldn't see what he was driving at.

"Uhhuh," he rumbled, "Well, now, supposing' that Baird was in the process o' windin' up his business as a blackmailer. He wasn't the sort o' man who'd just disappear an' leave his victims be. Not him. He'd think that, if he was foldin' the profession up, he might as well make a killin' on each victim. Say he went round to each o' 'em an' said, 'Look'ee here, I'm kinda reformed character. I'm kinda getting' out o' this dirty profession, an' I thought I'd be decent an' offer ye the proof which I ha' bin usin' against ye. Naturally, as I'm a poor man I can't do this for nothing', but tell ye what I'll do. I bin getting' a tenner a

month from ye. Well, I'll let ye have the proof which I hold
against ye for five hundred quid.' What d'ye say to that,
Max? If ye'd been in the position o' one of Baird's victims,
ye'd ha' bin only too pleased to help buy him out o'
business. It would be cheaper in the long run, an' ye'd feel
the whale o' a lot safer once ye'd lit the kitchen stove wi' the
damnin' evidence, wouldn't ye?"

I agreed. It seemed to me that the old man certainly had
something there. The only trouble was that I could not see
what immediate bearing it had on the murders.

In one spot (on pages118-119) blackmailer Baird is
described to us by another bookseller, who also talks a bit
about the, now very collectable, British gangster paperbacks
that began publication in the late 1940s and culminated with
the famous Hank Janson series, which were all the rage back
then:

I would hardly say, sir, that he was connected with the
trade. He was a scoundrel, sir, a dirty blackmailer. During
the war, bless you, sir, there were a lot of low characters
who crept into bookselling and publishing. It looked like a
good racket to them. They have mostly drifted out of the
trade again, sir, and good riddance to them says I. Baird
was mixed up in one of those wartime publishing rackets.
Their game, sir, was to publish cheap near pornography on
black market paper. They failed, sir. They didn't
understand the traditions of the trade. I knew all about
Baird, sir, bless you, as soon as I saw him. His racket was
the tough imitation American gangster thriller in which
girls have their clothes torn off. Harmless enough stuff, I
may say, sir, but I didn't like Baird. Since then, sir, he has
come out openly as a crook.

The case heats up as Max, The Professor and "The Bishop"
investigate the crime more deeply and question various

witnesses and suspects. The interplay between the three friends, each fellow unique and quite quirky in his own memorable way, makes for a fascinating mystery. Half the fun of the book is the interplay between this trio and our following them as they work out the facts and leads to discover the amazing identity of the murderer. It's like Holmes, Watson and Lestrade going on a marry chase to catch a murderer as they bicker and carp lovingly at each other.

The back cover blurbs of the Dover edition give a simple but concise description of this neglected classic:

Bodies In A Bookshop *is filled with amusing sallies of wit, quaint and pungent observations, droll characters and rambles among many a volume of forgotten lore. Crisp dialogue keeps the plot moving at top speed. After forty years,* Bodies In A Bookshop *is as exuberantly readable as ever, a welcome and refreshing relief from so many of today's flat and colorless mystery puzzles.*

And that says it better than ever I could. You don't come upon fine quirky novels like this any more, they're a rare treat, an acquired taste, and this one has a lot to offer. The Holmes and Watson link is definitely there in spirit, if not in deed. The mood, plot and characters offer much that any aficionado of Sherlock Holmes and Dr. Watson will find joyful and truly appreciate. The game is definitely afoot in this one!

The Alienist:
Sherlockian Formula Transmogrified

aleb Carr's best-selling Victorian era crime novel, *The Alienist*, is an exciting and fascinating novel. It is also an often-brutal crime novel about male child prostitution in New York City in 1896 as a haunting serial killer stalks these helpless children.

Aside from its gruesome but engrossing story, as I read this fine novel, I began to see numerous pieces of the Sherlock Holmes formula in the book. As a Holmes fan and reader, and author of a non-fiction bibliography on the books as well as the occasional pastiche — I could easily discern there was a Sherlockian formula at work here.

Dr. Laszlo Kreitzer, the European accented "alienist" of the title — or in more modern terms an early version of a forensic psychologist and profiler — is of course, a stand-in for Holmes. Kreitzer is dark, moody, mysterious, and at the same time manifests those obsessive tendencies, peculiarities, and sparks of genius we are aware of in our own beloved Sherlock. Laszlo Kreitzer is a compelling character. However, Kreitzer is not a beloved or loveable character and Carr keeps him more aloof and mysterious than Holmes ever was.

A look at the other characters in the book gives more evidence of the link to the Holmes stories. Where Doyle used Watson to great effect to show Holmes' below the surface essential decency and true humanity – Carr's *Times* reporter John Moore, hardly scratches the surface of his partner's true personality in his narration of the tale. Possibly an indication of some of the deficiencies of Carr as a writer –

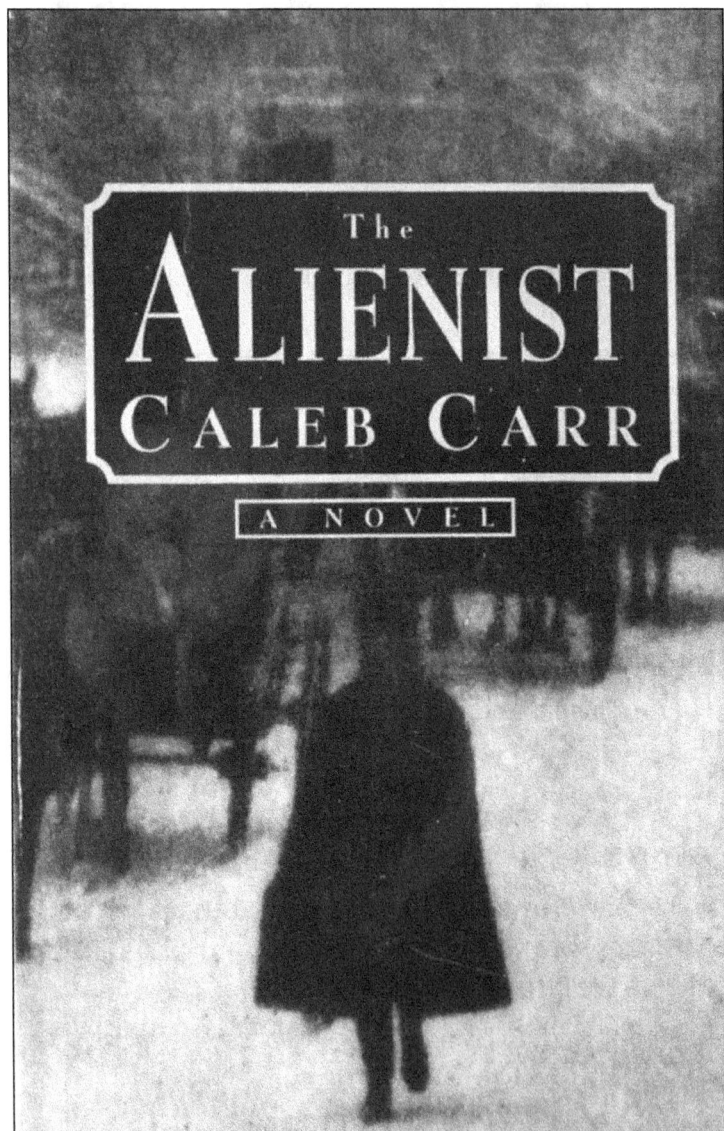

The
ALIENIST
CALEB CARR
A NOVEL

he's no Doyle – but then again, who is? But he's close. And in fact, Carr may not even be trying to emulate Sir Arthur or Holmes at all. Or perhaps it's just that his own characters can never hope to eclipse Holmes and Watson in any comparison. Such a comparison may not even be fair to Carr or his fine work at all.

John Moore is a good character and an adequate Watson type of narrator. He is an "average" man, much like Watson, engaged in momentous and dangerous events that scare him to his very being and that he does not fully understand. Moore looks to Kreitzer for information and explanations, just as Watson does to Holmes. Moore also exhibits those attributes, just as Watson does – as Holmes would say, in The Hound Of The Baskervilles to Watson: *"It may be that you are not yourself luminous, but you are a conductor of light. Some people without possessing genius have a remarkable power of stimulating it."*

So Moore is a very Watson-like character – but he is *not* Watson.

We also have Moore's long-suffering mother – whom he is living with on a temporary basis – very close shades of Mrs. Hudson there.

Then there's a host of interesting secondary characters Carr has woven into the fabric of the plot; the large black man named Cyrus; tiny Stevie Taggart, with shades of Wiggins; Mary, the husband killer; as well as policewoman wannabe Sara. Then there are the Detective Sergeant Issacson twins, and the New York City Police Commissioner, Theodore Roosevelt. It's a grand team of investigators and from their secret headquarters at 808 Broadway, they strive to uncover the reason for, and the perpetrator of, a series of truly horrendous murders of teen male prostitutes. The murders are particularly violent, mere butchery, and the killer is what would in our modern days be known as a serial killer. In the New York City of 1896 the mere existence of such a monster is not even dreamt of and there is no way to cope with such a fiend, muchless stop him. The city and its people lay helpless before him.

There is much investigation, supposition, and deduction in the grand Holmes manner about just what new kind of monster the team is up against. What kind of a killer is this and how was he spawned? There is much deduction about the formulation of a serial killer and early profiling that is fascinating. *Silence of the Lambs* meets *Ragtime* might be an off the cuff comparison.

The killer is truly an effective villain, aloof, mysterious, deadly, he taunts the police, Krietzer, and his team at every turn. He is a vicious, Ripper-type serial killer, but with a very different MO.

A dangerous cat and mouse game begins with the investigation – much as that engaged by Holmes with his greatest nemesis, Professor James Moriarity. There is also considerable political gamesmanship and back stabbing, and police department in fighting, as Krietzer, Moore, Roosevelt, and their agents, seek to solve the case. For instance, the Mayor, along with a group of thuggish ex-police and mysterious Catholic priests seek to do everything in their power to obstruct the investigation for their own cynical reasons.

By the middle of the book the killer, an ingenious serial murderer, has still not shown himself to the reader, much like Professor Moriarity's first appearance in the middle of the Holmes Canon.

Later on, Detective Sergeant Marcus Iassacson's analysis of the killer's note to a mother of one of the boy victims offers a bit of masterful deduction that Sherlock himself would have been proud of.

Victorian era New York City makes an effective backdrop for the story and makes for an interesting substitute for the foggy streets of Holmes' London. The book offers a good, detailed look at Victorian New York with some surprises in the depth and realization of vice back then.

All in all, *The Alienist* by Caleb Carr contains many of those elements that endear readers to the Holmes stories. It is, for want of a better word, Sherlockian formula transmogrified. The book is an effective mystery and serial killer novel. It is long, and the end left me a bit flat, as if Carr was really cooking along as he was writing the story, but then realized he had to end the damn thing somehow and do it soon. However, this is nitpicking. It's a fine novel, and I dare to say that it is an important one.

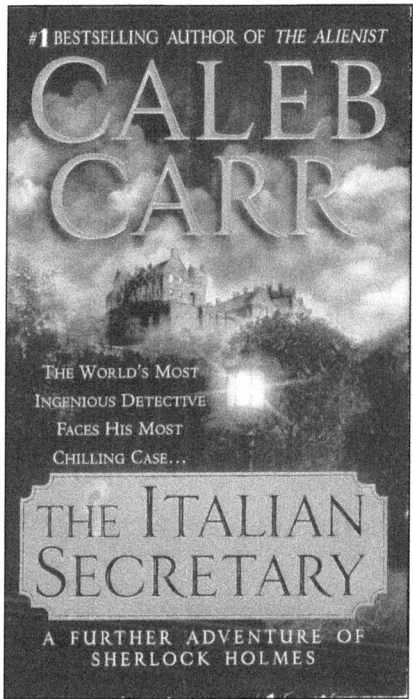

The book was a Random House hardcover from 1994 and a Bantam paperback from 1995. The hardcover shows a blurry and eerie photo detail from "The Street" by Alfred Strieglitz from *Camera Work*, July 1903. It was designed by Andy Carpenter, and sets the mood wonderfully. The paperback edition has a cover insert that shows the entire Victorian era photo, where the haunting image of what is supposed to be the killer gets lost in a bustling 1903 city scene. It is haunting and effective.

And, to taunt us even more, there is even a Holmes, who does appear! Though not what any fan would think, for he too is a transmogrification. In this case Holmes is actually Doctor H.H. Holmes, who was then executed for mass serial murders in Philadelphia.

Carr followed up the success of *The Alienist* with a sequel, *The Angel of Darkness* in 1997; and recently with, *The Alienist At Armageddon* in 2021. There is also a well-regarded TNT TV series of *The Alienist* that began in 2018 and is now in its third season.

So, with all this in mind, it seems only natural that Carr should write his own Sherlock Holmes pastiche novel. And he did that in 2005, with *The Italian Secretary* (Carroll & Graf hardcover; St. Martins Press, paperback in 2006). It is a fine Sherlockian outing in which Queen Victoria and the entire realm are placed in deadly danger. The Empire is in peril and Holmes and Watson are once again on the case!

So you can see how what I call Carr's transmogrified Sherlockian formula used in *The Alienist*, has gone full circle, with a fine Sherlock Holmes pastiche novel that is to the benefit of all fans of The Great Detective.

Watson: The Perfect Partner!

Did you ever wonder… ?
   Suppose Arthur Conan Doyle had *not* chosen Dr. Watson as the partner for Sherlock Holmes?

Doyle *could* have chosen someone else to partner with his Great Detective. It did not *have* to be Watson. So, if not Watson, then who else might fit the needs of Holmes as the perfect partner?

As Doyle was creating the character of Sherlock Holmes and was choosing a partner for his Great Detective, he knew he needed to pick someone who could showcase Holmes' unique talents to the world, but also a person who brought value to the relationship — someone who would be an important and intrinsic part of the Holmes team. And Holmes and Watson are a team, make no mistake about that! However, it was not all that easy for Holmes to find the right person to share rooms with, and get along with — or perhaps more importantly, someone who could get along with *him!*

"'I've found it! I've found it!' he shouted."
Geo. Hutchinson, *A Study in Scarlet* (London: Ward, Lock Bowden, and Co., 1891)

Holmes could be a difficult person to be around. He could be moody, arrogant, and troublesome. He kept odd hours. He test fired weapons indoors. He was also brilliant, but in a rather annoying way that most regular people would not accept or ever put up with for very long. Holmes was unique. Thus any person Holmes would share rooms with, must be

unique as well.

Sherlock Holmes also did not have *friends*, at least not in the way we commonly think of friends. His *friends* were more likely associates, a network of people used in his work to close cases; some members of the official police; criminals (reformed, such as Shinwell "Porky" Johnson, and others not reformed); the Baker Street Irregulars, even Toby the dog was a part of his 'team' at times.

With all that known, when Holmes was looking to share the rooms at 221B Baker Street with another person, he knew it must be someone who would be able to tolerate him and his odd manners — no easy feat — and more so, he wanted someone to be of value to him in his important work. The list would seem to be rather short, but there are some likely candidates.

Let us put Watson aside for the moment.

Holmes (through the writings of Doyle) could have chosen someone from another profession to be his partner. With that possibility in mind, is there someone other than Watson, or a medical doctor, who might have brought more to the table for Holmes?

There are other candidates, of course, other than good old Watson. Men of other important professions had much to offer. Perhaps a Scotland Yard Inspector? Or some young and talented constable? Perhaps a knowledgeable lawyer? A local politician? Or even a newspaper reporter? Men from each of these professions, or others, would bring experiences and contacts that would prove an important contribution to Holmes and his work.

Let's take a look at an official detective. Lestrade certainly would not be the man here, but another one of them might fit in well and have much to contribute to Holmes. A Scotland Yard Inspector could certainly grease the skids for Holmes with The Yard, and offer Holmes unique inside access to crime scenes, records, suspects, and all that! Perhaps? Or perhaps not, since early on in his career the official police did not understand nor respect

Holmes and his methods, nor appreciate what he was doing in his new consulting detective service. The feeling was mutual. Holmes looked upon the official police, including vaulted Scotland Yard Inspectors as plodding, unimaginative, incompetent and generally useless in solving crimes. The official police more often than not ignored or mucked-up key evidence at a crime scene — and sometimes even arrested the wrong man! No, there was no way that Holmes could ever share rooms with a member of the official police. He did not respect them — and they did not respect him — certainly not in the early days of his career.

Now a lawyer, or even a local politician might offer some good advice with the law or help in cutting red tape, and both would certainly have valued connections. However, Holmes did not need the advice of any lawyer to tell him why he could *not* take a certain action in his work. Nor did he need to listen to any self-serving politician. He did not trust or respect such men. Besides, he had Mycroft to turn to for any serious legal needs, or when he needed to access political juice.

However, as for Holmes sharing rooms with his brother, Mycroft, or teaming up with him — forget about that! They were brothers and sometimes associates, but they could never live together, nor be partners. They could barely tolerate each other!

Now a newspaper reporter might be an interesting choice. A competent writer and investigative journalist just might offer some positive contributions as a partner to Holmes, and a crime reporter even more so. The thought is intriguing. Even a muck-rake journalist of the so-called popular press might offer value by being able to reach into certain dark places, or contacting the right people to solve a crime. In fact, Doyle used exactly this device in the story of another of his famous heroes — newshound Malone in *The Lost World* played a definite Watson-like role as he told the story of Professor Challenger, and his unique talents and adventures.

However, Holmes did not need to room and partner with a newspaperman, as he had access to them quite readily when needed. He also had access to many of the same contacts any good newshound would have. So a newspaperman's qualities might actually be redundant. Also newspapermen could be very aggressive and such a man might reveal too much information, too soon, on his cases. Holmes could not abide that, so a journalist would not do.

So who then? For Holmes there is much to consider in choosing someone to share his work and life. This can be complicated because no one more than Holmes knows the dangers that a partner can be put in because of his line of work. Holmes deals with criminals and murderers all the time. These are enemies who would take revenge against him, and it is a fact he lives with every day. It is one reason, I believe, why Holmes does not involve himself romantically with the opposite sex. It is not because of some ill-gotten misogyny against women at all, in fact he loves and respects women — though he also knows they can be dangerous. Even deadly. However, Holmes knows that by becoming romantically involved with any woman, he would be forced to worry about her safety all the time. Holmes is aware any women he loved would always be in danger and his enemies would seek to target her — to get to him. Any child born from such a union would make the danger far worse! Such a situation was unconscionable. Holmes could never allow anyone he loved to be placed in such mortal danger. Certainly not a woman he loved. So he closed that part of his life. Holmes gave up a lot in the pursuit of his profession. However, he still needed to find someone to share the rooms at 221B with, and that person would have to be someone

special. Perhaps exceptional.

So what is it that makes Watson the perfect partner for Sherlock Holmes? We can trace the clues early on. They appear in the very first Sherlock Holmes story, "A Study in Scarlet". Here, even before Stamford introduces Watson to Holmes, he tells Watson he knows a man who is looking to share rooms. Watson replies:

"By Jove!" I cried, "if he really wants someone to share the rooms and the expense, I am the very man for him. I should prefer having a partner to being alone."

Already — even before he meets Holmes — Watson is thinking of Holmes as a potential *partner!* It is interesting that he uses that very word. However, in the very next paragraph of the story, Watson is warned.

"Young Stamford looked rather strangely at me over his wine-glass. "You don't know Sherlock Holmes yet," he said, "perhaps you would not care for him as a constant companion."

Once Watson is introduced to Holmes they speak about the rooms and the issue of compatibility comes up.

Sherlock Holmes seemed delighted at the idea of sharing his rooms with me.

"I have my eye on a suite in Baker Street," he said, "which would suit us down to the ground. You don't mind the smell of strong tobacco, I hope?"

"I always smoke 'ships" myself," I answered.

"That's good enough. I generally have chemicals about, and occasionally do experiments. Would that annoy you?"

"By no means."

"Let me see — what are my other shortcomings? I get in the dumps at times, and don't open my mouth for days on end. You must not think I am sulky when I do that. Just leave me alone, and I'll soon be right. What have you to confess now? It's just as well for two fellows to know the worst of one another before they begin to live together."

I laughed at this cross-examination. "I keep a bull pup." I *said. [*Never again mentioned by Watson, G.L.*]*, *"and I object to rows because my nerves are shaken, and I get up at all sorts of ungodly hours, and I am extremely lazy. I have another set of vices when I am well, but those are the principal ones at present."*

Holmes was looking for a man who would be able to put up with his unique eccentricities, but who can also contribute to his work. That is where Watson comes in. John Watson is a retired army medical doctor whose military medical knowledge adds significantly to Holmes own. In fact, Watson brings vast medical knowledge to the table - and while Holmes has a middling amount of knowledge in this area — Watson is an expert in the field and his opinion is invaluable to Holmes in the examination of bodies and determining time and mode of death.

DR. JOHN WATSON

Furthermore, Watson as a military man, has seen active service in the front lines in Afghanistan, a particularly brutal war. He has been wounded. He has treated the wounded on the battlefield. He has seen all types of serious injuries and bullet wounds. His medical knowledge is vast and deep and of inestimable value to Holmes — and Holmes knows it! Watson has seen war and action up close. He is brave and loyal. He still has his army service revolver — which Holmes is aware of and often asks him to carry along on dangerous cases. In other words, Holmes knows that Watson — who he can count on as a de facto enforcer — is brave and loyal and will not shirk at the sight of action or violence. Watson is steadfast. Watson can also take care of himself with a gun, he is not afraid to use it when necessary, and he is brave under fire. These are valuable assets to Holmes. He respects Watson's abilities.

However with Watson, Holmes gets much more. Watson is a good man, honest, trustworthy, he has a sense of humor, a well-rounded personality, and he is easy to be around. He is also a very decent fellow. The two men just naturally become good friends and get along well. These are character traits Holmes especially values, and they grow their relationship and friendship into a true partnership. And while Holmes took precautions when it came to Watson's safety, he had confidence in the doctor's ability to handle himself in any situation.

Furthermore, Watson is a writer, and he writes up Holmes cases and has them published in the popular press to world-wide acclaim. He does this to showcase his friend's great talent and unique abilities. While Holmes allows these published reports of his cases so as to popularize his methods as a consulting detective — he is also serious about these reports so that law enforcement can improve by learning his methods. Holmes even writes and publishes his own monographs upon certain aspects of detective work. His well-known study of cigarette ash is a detailed and highly instructive work allowing the reader to determine exactly what type of cigarette a criminal may have smoked just from the remains of the ash. Using this information, cigarette ash at a crime scene can offer an important clue in finding a killer. Furthermore, Holmes himself wrote at least one of his own cases for publication in *The Strand* magazine under Watson's name, ("The Adventure of The Lion's Mane", from 1907, but published in 1926). So we know that Holmes was not averse to having his methods, or knowledge of his cases made public, and Watson's write-ups of his cases fulfilled this desire admirably.

I believe, that no matter how much Holmes protested Watson's use of melodrama in the writing of some of his cases, The Great Detective secretly enjoyed the acclaim and attention Watson's chronicles brought him in the popular press. The writing and publication in *The Strand* of these cases by Watson warms Holmes' ego, it is a recognition of his life and work, and I believe it means more to Holmes than he would like to admit.

After Watson moves in with Holmes he comments on his new roommate in "A Study in Scarlet".

Holmes was certainly not a difficult man to live with. He was quiet in his ways, and his habits were regular. It was rare for him to be up after ten at night, and he had invariably breakfasted and gone out before I rose in the morning... Nothing could exceed his energy when the working fit was upon him, but now and again a reaction would seize him, and for days he would lie upon the sofa in the sitting-room, hardly uttering a word or moving a muscle from morning to night.

Obviously the two men are compatible. In the above statement Watson is being more than generous in his thoughts on life with Holmes. Their partnership and friendship grow over the years as Watson continually surprises Holmes with his loyalty, bravery, medical knowledge, and his writings of important cases — all of which show his devotion and admiration of Holmes. In fact, Holmes and Watson get along smashingly!

For Sherlock Holmes — there surely is no other choice — Watson is the perfect partner!

Gary Lovisi Bibliography

Sherlock Holmes:
The Secret Adventures of Sherlock Holmes Series:
The Secret Adventures of Sherlock Holmes (Ramble House, 2007)
More Secret Adventures of Sherlock Holmes (Ramble House, 2011)
Secret Adventures of Sherlock Holmes: Book Three (Ramble House, 2016)
More Secret Files of Sherlock Holmes (Linford, UK, 2017)

Souvenirs of Sherlock Holmes (Gryphon Books, 2002; non-fiction)
Sherlock Holmes: The Great Detective in Paperback & Pastiche (Gryphon Books, 2008)
Sherlock Holmes: The Baron's Revenge (Airship27, 2012)
The Mystery Surrounding Watson's Lost Dispatch Box (MX Pub., UK, 2014)
Happy Birthday, Mr. Holmes (Gryphon Books, 2016)
The Affair of Lady Westcott's Lost Ruby & The Case of The Unseen Assassin (Black Gat #11, 2017; novellas)
Sherlock Holmes in Oz (Wildside Press, 2022)

Crime:
Extreme Measures (Gryphon Books, 1996; stories)
Ultra-Boiled: Hard Hitting Crime Fiction (Ramble House, 2010; stories)
Murder of a Bookman (Wildside Press, 2011)
Driving Hell's Highway (Wildside Press, 2011)
The Nemesis Chronicles (Bold Venture, 2016; stories)

Griff & Fats series
Hellbent on Homicide (Do Not Press, UK, 1997)
Harvest of Homicide (Bold Venture Press, 2017)
Hardcases & Homicide (Bold Venture Press, 2022)

Vic Powers series
Dirty Dogs (Gryphon Books, 1999; stories)
Blood in Brooklyn (Do Not Press, UK, 1999)
Violence is the Only Solution (Wildside Press, 2012; stories)
The Last Goodbye (Bold Venture, 2015)

Science Fiction /
Fantasy & Horror:
Sarasha (Gryphon Books, 1997)
Gargoyle Nights
  (Wildside Press, 2011; stories)
Mars Needs Books
  (Wildside Press, 2011)
When the Dead Walk
  (Ramble House, 2014)

The Jon Kirk of Ares Series:
  (Wildside Press)
#1 The Winged Men (2014)
#2 The Invisible Men (2015)
#3 The Space Men (2015)
#4 The Mind Masters (2017)
#5 The Time Masters (2017)

Other Fiction:
West Texas War and Other Western
  Stories (Ramble House, 2007)
The Sicilian, Book 1: Augustus the
  Undefeated (Wildside Press,
  2017)
The Sicilian, Book 2: Augustus the
  Conqueror (Wildside Press, 2022)

Edited Anthologies:
The Great Detective: His Further
  Adventures (Wildside Press,
  2012)
Battling Boxing Stories
  (Wildside Press, 2012)

Non-Fiction:
The Sexy Digests
  (Gryphon Books, 2001)
The Swedish Vintage Paperback
  Guide (Gryphon Books, 2003)
The Pulp Crime Digests
  (Gryphon Books, 2004)
Modern Historical Adventure
  Novels (Gryphon Books, 2006)
The Antique Trader Paperback
  Price Guide
  (Krauss Books, 2008)
Dames, Dolls & Delinquents
  (Krauss Books, 2009)
Bad Girls Need Love Too
  (Krauss Books, 2010)

About the Author

GARY LOVISI is an author who has done work in many genres, with fiction and non-fiction. He has been a reader, fan and book collector for most of his life. He is a Mystery Writers of America, Edgar Award Nominated author for his Sherlock Holmes pastiche story, "The Adventure of the Missing Detective". His latest book is the novel, *Sherlock Holmes in Oz* (Wildside Press, 2022), that brings together these two iconic characters and worlds into an amazing missing person adventure. Lovisi has been a popular contributor to *Sherlock Holmes Mystery Magazine* (including with his Holmes / Challenger team-up story, "Challenger's Titanic Challenge", issue #12); as well as appearing in three anthologies from St. Martins Press, edited by Michael Kurland. He has also written *Sherlock Holmes: The Baron's Revenge* (Airship27, tpb), which is a sequel to the original Holmes story by Doyle, "The Illustrious Client". Lovisi has written three books in *The Secret Adventures of Sherlock Holmes* series (Ramble House Books), and two of his Inspector Mac and Holmes team-up adventures appear in Stark House Press's Black Gat Book #11. His Sherlockian non-fiction has appeared in *Souvenirs of Sherlock Holmes*, *Relics of Sherlock Holmes*, and *Sherlock Holmes: The Great Detective In Paperback & Pastiche*. Lovisi is also the editor and publisher of the popular book collector magazine, *Paperback Parade*, which he has published since 1986 and is now in it's 35th year of publication!

You can find out more about Lovisi and his work at his website: www.gryphonbooks.com, and through his Facebook page. Also check out his *YouTube* videos on all types of collectable books and related items.

Photo by Laura Cali

www.ingramcontent.com/pod-product-compliance
Lightning Source LLC
Chambersburg PA
CBHW062134020426
42335CB00013B/1217